VOLCANOES

Eruptions and Other Volcanic Hazards

THE HAZARDOUS EARTH

VOLCANOES

Eruptions and Other Volcanic Hazards

Timothy Kusky, Ph.D.

Facts On File
An imprint of Infobase Publishing

VOLCANOES: Eruptions and Other Volcanic Hazards

Facts On File, Inc.
An imprint of Infobase Publishing
132 West 31st Street
New York NY 10001

Library of Congress Cataloging-in-Publication Data

Kusky, Timothy M.
    Volcanoes: eruptions and other volcanic hazards / Timothy Kusky.
        p. cm.—(The hazardous earth)
    Includes bibliographical references and index.
    ISBN-13: 978-0-8160-6463-2
    ISBN-10: 0-8160-6463-6
    1. Volcanoes. I. Title.
    QE522.K87 2008
    551.21—dc22   2007022342

Facts On File books are available at special discounts when purchased in bulk quantities for businesses, associations, institutions, or sales promotions. Please call our Special Sales Department in New York at (212) 967-8800 or (800) 322-8755.

You can find Facts On File on the World Wide Web at http://www.factsonfile.com

Text design by Erika K. Arroyo
Illustrations by Richard Garratt and Melissa Ericksen
Photo research by Suzanne M. Tibor

Printed in the United States of America

VB ML 10 9 8 7 6 5 4 3 2 1

This book is printed on acid-free paper and contains 30 percent post-consumer recycled content.

To Dabney Caldwell,
1927–2006

■ ■ ■

Contents

Preface

Natural geologic hazards arise from the interaction between humans and the Earth's natural processes. Recent natural disasters such as the 2004 Indian Ocean tsunami that killed more than a quarter million people and earthquakes in Iran, Turkey, and Japan have shown how the motion of the Earth's tectonic plates can suddenly make apparently safe environments dangerous or even deadly. The slow sinking of the land surface along many seashores has made many of the world's coastal regions prone to damage by ocean storms, as shown disastrously by Hurricane Katrina in 2005. Other natural Earth hazards arise gradually, such as the migration of poisonous radon gas into people's homes. Knowledge of the Earth's natural hazards can lead one to live a safer life, providing guidance on where to build homes, where to travel, and what to do during natural hazard emergencies.

The eight-volume The Hazardous Earth set is intended to provide middle- and high-school students and college students with a readable yet comprehensive account of natural geologic hazards—the geologic processes that create conditions hazardous to humans—and what can be done to minimize their effects. Titles in the set present clear descriptions of plate tectonics and associated hazards, including earthquakes, volcanic eruptions, landslides, and soil and mineral hazards, as well as hazards resulting from the interaction of the ocean, atmosphere, and land, such as tsunamis, hurricanes, floods, and drought. After providing the reader with an in-depth knowledge of naturally hazardous processes, each volume gives vivid accounts of historic disasters and events that have shaped human history and serve as reminders for future generations.

One volume covers the basic principles of plate tectonics and earthquake hazards, and another volume covers hazards associated with volcanoes. A third volume is about tsunamis and related wave phenomena, and another volume covers landslides, soil, and mineral hazards, and includes discussions of mass wasting processes, soils, and the dangers of the natural concentration of hazardous elements such as radon. A fifth volume covers hazards resulting from climate change and drought, and how they affect human populations. That volume also discusses glacial environments and landforms, shifting climates, and desertification—all related to the planet's oscillations from ice ages to hothouses. Greater understanding is achieved by discussing environments on Earth that resemble icehouse (glaciers) and hothouse (desert) conditions. A sixth volume, entitled *The Coast,* includes discussion of hazards associated with hurricanes, coastal subsidence, and the impact of building along coastlines. A seventh volume, *Floods,* discusses river flooding and flood disasters, as well as many of the contemporary issues associated with the world's diminishing freshwater supply in the face of a growing population. This book also includes a chapter on sinkholes and phenomena related to water overuse. An eighth volume, *Asteroids and Meteorites,* presents information on impacts that have affected the Earth, their effects, and the chances that another impact may occur soon on Earth.

The Hazardous Earth set is intended overall to be a reference book set for middle school, high school, and undergraduate college students, teachers and professors, scientists, librarians, journalists, and anyone who may be looking for information about Earth processes that may be hazardous to humans. The set is well illustrated with photographs and other illustrations, including line art, graphs, and tables. Each volume stands alone and can also be used in sequence with other volumes of the set in a natural hazards or disasters curriculum.

Acknowledgments

Many people have helped me with different aspects of preparing this volume. I would especially like to thank Carolyn, my wife, and my children, Shoshana and Daniel, for their patience during the long hours spent at my desk preparing this book. Without their understanding this work would not have been possible. Frank Darmstadt, executive editor, reviewed and edited all text and figures, providing guidance and consistency throughout. Photo researcher Suzanne M. Tibor proved an invaluable asset in finding a number of interesting and compelling photos for this volume. Many sections of the work draw from my own experiences doing scientific research in different parts of the world, and it is not possible to thank the hundreds of colleagues whose collaborations and work I have related in this book. Their contributions to the science that allowed the writing of this volume are greatly appreciated. I have tried to reference the most relevant works or, in some cases, more recent sources that have more extensive reference lists. Any omissions are unintentional.

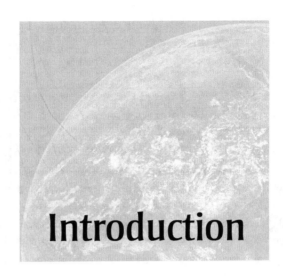

Introduction

Volcanic eruptions provide one of the most spectacular of all natural phenomena, yet they also rank among the most dangerous of geological hazards. More than 500 million people worldwide live near active volcanoes and need to understand the risks associated with volcanic eruptions and how to respond in the event of volcanic emergencies. Eruptions may send blocks of rock, ash, and gas tens of thousands of feet into the atmosphere in beautiful eruption plumes, yet individual eruptions have also killed tens of thousands of people. The hazards associated with volcanic eruptions are not limited to the immediate threat from the flowing *lava* and ash, but include longer-term atmospheric and climate effects and changes to land use patterns and the livelihoods of human populations.

People have been awed by the power and fury of volcanoes for thousands of years, as evidenced by biblical passages referring to eruptions and, more recently, by the destruction of Pompeii and Herculaneum from the eruption of Italy's Mount Vesuvius in the year 79 C.E. (Current, or Common, Era). Sixteen thousand people died in Pompeii alone, buried by a fast-moving hot incandescent ash flow known as a *nuée ardent.* This famous eruption buried Pompeii in thick ash that quickly solidified, which preserved the city and its inhabitants remarkably well. In the 16th century, Pompeii was rediscovered and has since been the focus of archaeological investigations. Mount Vesuvius is still active, looming over the present-day city of Naples, Italy. Most residents of Naples rarely think about the threat looming over their city. There are many apparently dormant volcanoes similar to Vesuvius around the world, and people who live near them need to understand the potential threats and hazards posed by these sleeping giants to know how to react in the event of a major eruption.

Volcanoes examines the different types of volcanic eruptions, starting with an introduction to volcanoes, volcanic landforms, and *plate tectonics*, followed by a fairly detailed description of the various characteristics of magma that lead to differences in eruption style. The first chapter in the book also includes discussion of the classification of igneous rocks and the different physical processes deep within the Earth that lead to the formation of different types of magma, volcanic eruption style, and igneous rocks. The last part of the first chapter consists of a discussion of different types of volcanic rocks, landforms, eruptions, and the tectonic settings that typically host each type of eruption. Chapter 2 examines the extreme hazards associated with volcanism, including the eruption cloud, poisonous gases, volcanic flows, mudflows, floods, and debris avalanches. *Tsunamis* and *earthquakes* are covered, and the chapter ends with an analysis of the long-range consequences of volcanic eruptions in terms of changes in climate. Chapter 3 discusses the prediction of eruptions and methods to reduce or mitigate volcanic disasters once the hazards of individual volcanoes are known. In-depth discussions of historical eruptions in chapter 4 illustrate each of these hazards and events that let the hazards become disasters.

At certain times in Earth's history huge amounts of volcanism have covered vast areas with lava flows, and the consequences of the release of so many volcanic gases include changes to the planetary atmosphere and the course of life on Earth. Chapter 5 examines these and other rare types of massive and extremely violent volcanic eruptions, and their consequences in terms of the evolution of life on Earth are discussed in chapter 6. It is now recognized that an impact with a space object, probably a meteorite, caused the extinction of the dinosaurs and 65 percent of the other species on the planet at the end of the Cretaceous period 66 million years ago. The impact occurred at a time when the world's biosphere was already stressed, probably by massive amounts of volcanism and sea-level fall. The volcanic fields from this time are preserved as vast lava plains in western India known as the Deccan traps and on the Seychelles and other islands in the Indian Ocean. Impacts and massive volcanism can both dramatically change the global climate on scales that far exceed the changes witnessed in the past few thousands of years. These changes have dramatic influences on evolution and extinction of species, and current ideas suggest that impacts and volcanism have been responsible for most of the great extinctions of geological time. Other rare geologic events may be less dramatic than meteorite impacts, though still beyond the scale of anything we have seen on Earth in recent times. One example of this "extreme" geology is the formation of *kimberlite* pipes, which are large volcanic pipes that come from deep in the Earth and explode their way to the surface with such force that they may blow holes through the stratosphere. These kimberlite pipes carry diamonds from hundreds of kilometers in the Earth and seem to form in places that were abnormally rich in fluids. The global effect of kimberlites is not known, but you certainly would not want to be in the vicinity when one punches through the crust. The local effects of these kimberlite explosions are thought to resemble the destruction wrought by nuclear blasts, with large areas of widespread devastation around the kimberlite intrusion pipes.

1

Plate Tectonics, Volcanoes, and Igneous Rocks

The planet Earth formed about 4.5 billion years ago during the condensation of the solar nebula that left our present solar system with eight main planets circling the sun. Until recently, a ninth and distant object, Pluto, was regarded as a planet as well, but an astronomical conference in 2006 voted that this orbiting body did not meet the size and other criteria to warrant its designation as a planet. During its formation, the Earth was differentiated into several layers, including an outermost layer called the crust, consisting mostly of minerals made from light elements such as silicon (Si) and oxygen (O_2) forming an outer shell that is 3–50 miles (5–70 km) thick. This is followed inwardly by the mantle, a solid rocky layer that has minerals made from heavier elements such as magnesium (Mg) and iron (Fe), extending to 1,800 miles (2,900 km) beneath the surface. Next comes the outer core, which is a molten metallic layer extending to 3,200 miles (5,100 km) depth, and last is the inner core, a solid metallic layer extending to 3,950 miles (6,370 km) at the center of the Earth.

Plate Tectonics

Plate tectonics is a relatively new theory in the earth sciences, and this theory proposes that the outer shells of the Earth are divided into many different rigid plates that are all moving in relation to one another. This outer rigid layer is known as the *lithosphere,* which is the Greek word for rigid rock sphere. The lithosphere ranges from 45 to 100 miles

(75–150 km) thick. The lithosphere is essentially floating on a denser, but partially molten and weaker, layer of rock in the upper mantle known as the *asthenosphere* (the Greek word for "weak sphere"). It is the weakness of this layer that allows the plates on the surface of Earth to move about.

The tectonic plates are rigid and do not deform internally when they move, only along their edges. The edges are therefore where most mountain ranges are located and where most of the world's earthquakes occur and active volcanoes are located. There are only three fundamental types of plate boundaries. *Divergent boundaries* are where two plates move apart, creating a void that is typically filled by new magma that solidifies to form oceanic crust that wells up to fill the progressively opening hole. *Convergent boundaries* are where two plates move toward each other, resulting in one plate sliding beneath the other when a dense oceanic plate is involved, or *collision* and deformation, when continental plates are involved. Lines of volcanoes, known as *volcanic arcs,* or *magmatic arcs,* form above these sinking plates, resting on the edge of the overriding plate. *Transform boundaries* form where two plates slide past each other, such as along the San Andreas Fault in California, and typically have few volcanoes.

Where plates diverge, *seafloor spreading* produces new oceanic crust, as volcanic *basalt* pours out of the depths of Earth, filling the gaps generated by the moving plates. Examples of where this can be seen on the surface include Iceland along the Rekjanes Ridge. Beneath the Rekjanes and other oceanic ridges, magma rises from depth in the mantle and forms chambers filled with magma just below the crest of the ridges. The magma in these chambers erupts out through cracks in the roof of the chambers and forms extensive lava flows on the surface. As the two different plates on either side of the magma chamber move apart, these lava flows continuously fill in the gap between the diverging plates, creating new oceanic crust.

Oceanic lithosphere is being destroyed by sinking back into the mantle at the deep ocean trenches, in a process called *subduction.* As the oceanic slabs go down, they experience higher temperatures that cause rock-melts or magmas to be generated, which then move upward to intrude the overlying plate. Since subduction zones are long narrow zones where large plates are being subducted into the mantle, the melting produces a long line of volcanoes above the down-going plate and forms a volcanic arc. Depending on what the overriding plate is made of, this arc may be built on either a continental or on an oceanic plate.

Volcanoes and Plate Tectonics

Most volcanic eruptions on the planet are associated with the boundaries of tectonic plates. Extensional or divergent plate boundaries where plates are being pulled apart such as along the *mid-ocean ridges* have the greatest volume of magma erupted each year for any volcanic province on the Earth. However, these eruptions are not generally hazardous, especially since most of them occur many miles (km) below sea level. A few exceptions to this rule are noted where the mid-ocean ridges rise above sea level, such as in Iceland. There, volcanoes including the famous Hekla volcano have caused significant damage. Hekla has even erupted beneath a glacier, causing instant melting and generating fast-moving catastrophic floods called *jökulhlaups.* Despite these hazards, Icelanders have learned to benefit from living in a volcanically active area, tapping a large amount of heat in geothermal power generating systems.

Larger volcanoes are associated with extensional plate boundaries located in continents. For instance, the east African *rift* system is where the African continent is being ripped apart, and it hosts some

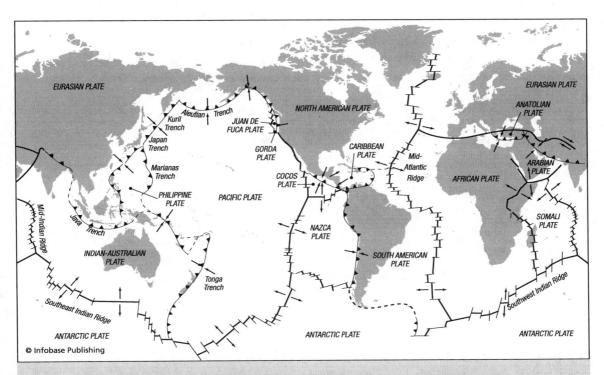

Map of the Earth showing major plate boundaries and locations of active volcanoes

spectacular volcanic cones, including Kilimanjaro, Ol Doinyo Lengai, Nyiragongo, and many others.

The most hazardous volcanoes on the planet are associated with convergent plate boundaries, where one plate is sliding beneath another in a subduction zone. The famous *Ring of Fire* rims the Pacific Ocean and refers to the ring of abundant volcanoes located above subduction zones around the Pacific Ocean. The Ring of Fire extends through the western Americas, Alaska, Kamchatka, Japan, Southeast Asia, and Indonesia. Volcanoes in this belt, including Mount Saint Helens in Washington State, typically have violent explosive eruptions that have killed many people and altered the landscape over wide regions.

An unusual style of volcanic activity is not associated with plate boundaries, but instead forms large broad volcanic shields in the interior of plates. These volcanoes typically have spectacular but not extremely explosive eruptions. The most famous of these "intraplate" volcanoes is Mauna Loa on Hawaii. Hazards associated with these volcanoes include lava flows and traffic jams from tourists trying to see the flows.

Why is there such a variation in the style of volcanic eruptions, and what causes specific types of eruptions to be associated with different types of plate boundaries? The next section examines the different types of magmas and eruptions in some detail in order to answer these questions, which is essential for planning how to respond to volcanic hazards in different parts of the world.

Different Kinds of Igneous Rocks

Molten rock that reaches the surface of the Earth is known as *magma*. When the magma reaches the surface, it is known as lava, which may flow or explosively erupt from volcanoes. The wide variety of eruption styles and hazards associated with volcanoes around the world can be linked to variations in several factors, including

- different types of magma, the name for molten rock within the Earth
- different types of gases in the magma
- different volumes of magma
- different forces of eruption
- different areas that are affected by each eruption

Different types of magma form in distinct tectonic settings, explaining many of the differences above. Other distinctions between eruption style are explained by the variations in processes that occur in the

Photo of volcanic igneous rock showing large potassium feldspar phenocrysts in a fine-grained matrix *(USGS)*

Photo of plutonic igneous rock (granite) showing overall coarse-grain size *(USGS)*

magma as it makes its way from deep within the Earth to the surface at a volcanic vent.

Most magma solidifies below the surface, forming *igneous rocks* (*igneous* is the Latin word for "fire"). Igneous rocks that form below the surface are called intrusive or *plutonic* rocks, whereas those that crystallize on the surface are called extrusive or volcanic rocks. Rocks that crystallize at a very shallow depth are called *hypabyssal* rocks. Some common plutonic rock types include granites, and some of the most abundant volcanic rocks include basalts and rhyolites. Intrusive igneous rocks crystallize slowly, giving crystals an extended time to grow, thus forming rocks with large mineral grains that are clearly distinguishable to the naked eye. These rocks are called phanerites. In contrast, magma that cools rapidly forms fine-grained rocks. Aphanites are igneous rocks in which the component grains cannot be distinguished readily without a microscope and are formed when magma from a volcano falls or flows across the surface and cools quickly. Some igneous rocks, known as porphyries, have two distinct populations of grain size. One group of very large crystals (called phenocrysts) is mixed with a uniform groundmass or matrix filling the space between the large crystals. This indicates two stages of cooling, as when magma has resided for a long time beneath a volcano, growing big crystals. When the volcano erupts it spews out a mixture of the large crystals and liquid magma that then cools quickly, forming the phenocrysts and the fine-grained groundmass.

Naming Igneous Rocks

Determining whether an igneous rock is phaneritic or aphanitic is just the first stage in giving it a name. The second stage is determining its chemical constituents. The composition of magma is controlled by the most abundant elements in the Earth, including silicon (Si), aluminum (Al), iron (Fe), calcium (Ca), magnesium (Mg), sodium (Na), potassium (K), hydrogen (H), and oxygen (O). Oxygen is the most abundant ion so we usually express compositional variations of magmas in terms of oxides. For most magmas, the largest constituent is represented by the combination of one silicon atom with two oxygen atoms, forming silicon dioxide, more commonly called silica. There are three very narrow compositional variations in the silica content of magma that are very common. The first type has about 50 percent silica (SiO_2), the second 60 percent, and the third 70 percent. We call these volcanic rock types basalt, andesite, and rhyolite, and the corresponding plutonic rocks gabbro, *granodiorite,* and *granite.* The table on page 7 shows the different kinds of igneous rocks.

Some of the variation in the nature of different types of volcanic eruptions can be understood by examining what causes magmas to have such a wide range in composition.

Magma Types			
	SiO$_2$ %	VOLCANIC ROCK	PLUTONIC ROCK
mafic	45–52%	basalt	gabbro
intermediate	53–65%	andesite	diorite
felsic	65%	rhyolite	granite

Extrusive Igneous Rocks

Magma that reaches the Earth's surface and flows as hot streams or is explosively blown out of a volcano is called lava. Lava has a range of compositions, a variety of high temperatures, and flows at various speeds.

The chemical composition of a magma is closely related to how explosive and hazardous a volcanic eruption will be. The variation in the amount of silica (SiO$_2$) in igneous rocks is used to describe the variation in composition of igneous rocks—and the magmas that formed them. Rocks with low amounts of silica (basalt, gabbro) are known as mafic rocks, whereas rocks with high concentrations of silica (rhyolite, granite) are known as silicic or felsic rocks.

All magmas have a small amount of gas dissolved in them, usually comprising between 0.2 and 3 percent of the magma volume, and this is typically water vapor and carbon dioxide. The gases typically control such features as how explosive a volcanic eruption can be with greater abundances of gases leading to more explosive eruptions.

Magmas have a wide range in temperatures. It is difficult to directly measure the temperature of an erupting volcano, since temperatures typically exceed 930°F (500°C) and melt most thermometers or the volcano may explode, killing the people trying to measure its temperature. Therefore, temperature is measured from a distance using optical devices, yielding temperatures in the range of 1,900–2,200°F (1,040–1,200°C) for basaltic magma and as low as 1,155°F (625°C) for some rhyolitic magmas.

Magmas move downhill at variable rates. For example, in Hawaii magma often flows downhill in magma streams at about 10 MPH (16 km/hr), destroying whole neighborhoods, whereas in other places it may move downhill so slowly as to be hardly detectable. At the other end of the spectrum, some explosive volcanic ash clouds move downhill at speeds of several hundred miles (km) per hour, destroying everything in their path. The measure of the resistance to flow of a magma is called *viscosity*. The more viscous a magma, the less fluid it is. Molasses is more viscous than water. The viscosity of magma depends on its temperature and composition. Higher temperature magma such as basalt tends to have a higher fluidity (lower viscosity) than lower temperature magma such as rhyolite, explaining why basaltic flows tend to move over large distances whereas rhyolitic magmas form large steep-sided domes around the volcanic vent they erupted from. Magmas with more silica in them (like rhyolite) are more resistant to flow because the silica molecule forms bonds with other atoms (mostly oxygen) that form large chains and rings of molecules that offer more resistance to flow than magmas without these large interlocking molecules.

Intrusive Igneous Bodies

Once magmas are formed from melting rocks deep within the Earth, they rise to intrude the crust and may take several forms. A "pluton" is a general name for a large cooled igneous intrusive body in the Earth. The name of the specific type of pluton is based on its geometry, size, and relations to the older rocks surrounding the pluton, known as country rock. Concordant plutons have boundaries parallel to layering in the country rock, whereas discordant plutons have boundaries that cut

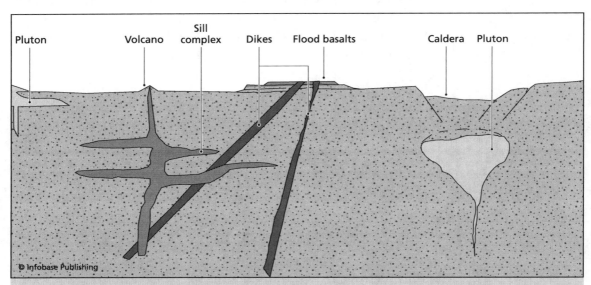

Forms of intrusive igneous rocks, including plutons, dikes, sills, and related structures

Photo of Devils Tower volcanic neck, Wyoming, showing spectacular columnar joints (*T. Kusky*)

across layering in the country rock. *Dikes* are tabular but discordant intrusions, and sills are tabular and concordant intrusive rocks. Volcanic necks are conduits connecting a volcano with its underlying magma chamber. A famous example of a volcanic neck is Devils Tower in Wyoming. Some plutons are so large that they have special names. Batholiths have a surface area of more than 60 square miles (100 sq km).

Batholiths contain hundreds to thousands of cubic miles of formerly molten magma, being more than 60 square miles (100 sq km) on the surface and typically extending many miles deep. Scientists have long speculated on how such large volumes of magma intrude the crust, and what relationships these magmas have on the style of volcanic eruption. One mechanism that may operate is assimilation, where the hot magma melts surrounding country rocks as it rises, causing them to become part of the magma. In doing this, the magma becomes cooler, and its composition changes to reflect the added melted country rock. Most geologists think that magmas may rise only a very limited distance by the process of assimilation. Some magmas may forcefully push their way into the crust if there are high pressures in the magma. One variation of this forceful emplacement style is *diapirism,* where the weight of surrounding rocks pushes down on the melt layer, which squeezes its way up through cracks that can expand and extend, forming volcanic vents at the surface. Stoping is a mechanism whereby big blocks get thermally shattered and drop off the top of the magma chamber and fall into the chamber, much like a glass ceiling breaking and falling into the space below.

The Origin of Magma

Magmas come from deep within the Earth, but what conditions lead to the generation of melts in the interior of the Earth? The temperature generally increases with depth in the Earth, since the surface is cool and the interior is hot. The *geothermal gradient* is a measure of how temperature increases with depth in the Earth, and it provides information about the depths at which melting occurs and the depths at which magmas form. The differences in the composition of the oceanic and continental crusts lead to differing abilities to conduct the heat from the interior of the Earth, and thus different geothermal gradients. The geothermal gradients show that temperatures within the Earth quickly exceed 1,830°F (1,000°C) with depth, so why are these rocks not molten? The answer is that pressures are very high, and pressure influences the ability of a rock to melt. As the pressure rises, the temperature at which the rock melts also rises. However, this effect of pressure on melting is modified greatly by the presence of water, because wet minerals melt at lower temperatures than dry minerals. As the pressure rises, the amount of water that can be dissolved in a melt also increases. Therefore, increasing the pressure on a wet mineral has the opposite effect as increasing the pressure on a dry mineral: It decreases the melting temperature.

If a rock melts completely, the magma has the same composition as the rock. Rocks are made of many different minerals, all of which melt at different temperatures. Therefore, if a rock is slowly heated, the resulting melt or magma will first have the composition of the first mineral that melts. If the rock melts further, the melt will have the composition of the first plus the second minerals that melt, and so on. If the rock continues to completely melt, the magma will eventually end up with the same composition as the starting rock, but this does not always happen. What often occurs is that the rock only partially melts, so that the minerals with low melting temperatures contribute to the magma, whereas the minerals with high melting temperatures did not melt and are left as a residue (called a restite). In this way, the end magma can have a composition different than the rock it came from.

The phrase "magmatic *differentiation* by partial melting" refers to the process of forming magmas with differing compositions through the incomplete melting of rocks. For magmas formed in this way, the composition of the magma depends on both the composition of the parent rock and the percentage of melt.

BASALTIC MAGMA

Partial melting in the mantle leads to the production of basaltic magma, which forms most of the oceanic crust. By looking at the mineralogy of the oceanic crust, which is dominated by the minerals olivine (Mg_2SiO_4), pyroxene ($Mg,FeSi_2O_6$), and feldspar ($KAlSi_3O_8$), we conclude that very little water is involved in the production of the oceanic crust. These minerals are all anhydrous, that is without water in their structure. Therefore, partial melting of the upper mantle without the presence of water must lead to the formation of oceanic crust. By collecting samples of the mantle that have been erupted through volcanoes, we know that it has a composition of garnet *peridotite* (olivine + garnet + orthopyroxene). By taking samples of this back to the laboratory and raising the temperature and pressure so that they are equal to 60 miles (100 km) depth, experiments show that 10 percent to 15 percent partial melt of this garnet peridotite yields a basaltic magma.

Magma that forms at 60 miles (100 km) depth is less dense than the surrounding solid rock, so it rises, sometimes quite rapidly (at rates of half a mile (1 km) per day measured by earthquakes under Hawaii). In fact, it may rise so fast that it does not cool off appreciably, erupting at the surface at more than 1,830°F (1,000°C). That is where basalt comes from.

GRANITIC MAGMA

Granitic magmas are very different from basaltic magmas. They have about 20 percent more silica, and the minerals in granite include quartz (SiO_2) and the complex minerals mica (K,Na,Ca) $(Mg,Fe,Al)_2AlSi_4O_{10}$ $(OH,F)_2$ and amphibole $((Mg,Fe,Ca)_2$ $(Mg,Fe,Al)_5$ $(Si,Al)_8$ O_{22} $(OH)_2)$, which both have a lot of water in their crystal structures. Also, granitic magmas are found almost exclusively in regions of continental crust. From these observations we infer that the source of granitic magmas is within the continental crust. Laboratory experiments suggest that when rocks with the composition of continental crust start to melt at temperature and pressure conditions found in the lower crust, a granitic liquid is formed, with 30 percent partial melting. These rocks can begin to melt by either the addition of a heat source such as basalt intruding the lower continental crust or released lowering the melting temperature by adding water from hydrous minerals buried to these depths.

These granitic magmas rise slowly because of their high SiO_2 and high viscosities until they reach the level in the crust where the temperature and pressure conditions are consistent with freezing or solidification of magma with this composition. This is about 3–6 miles (5–10 km) beneath the surface, which explains why large portions of the continental crust are not molten lava lakes. There are many regions with crust above large magma bodies (called batholiths) that are heated by the cooling magma. An example is Yellowstone National Park, where there are hot springs, geysers, and many features indicating that there is a large hot magma body at depth. Much of Yellowstone Park is a giant valley called a *caldera*, formed when an ancient volcanic eruption emptied an older batholith of its magma and the overlying crust collapsed into the empty hole formed by the eruption.

ANDESITIC MAGMA

The average composition of the continental crust is andesitic, or somewhere between the composition of basalt and rhyolite. Laboratory experiments show that partial melting of wet oceanic crust yields an andesitic magma. Most andesites today are erupted along continental margin convergent boundaries where a slab of oceanic crust is subducted beneath the continent. Remember that oceanic crust is dry, but after it forms it interacts with seawater, which fills cracks to several miles depth. Also, the sediments on top of the oceanic crust are full of water, but these are for the large part non-subductable. Andesite forms above places where water is released from the subducted slabs, and it migrates up into the mantle wedge above the subducting slab, forming water-rich magmas. These magmas then intrude the continental crust above, some forming volcanic andesites, others crystallizing as plutons of diorite at depth.

SOLIDIFICATION OF MAGMA

Just as rocks partially melt to form different liquid compositions, magmas may solidify to different minerals at different times to form different

(opposite page) Cross sections across convergent plate boundaries showing volcanic arcs forming by partial melting above subduction zones

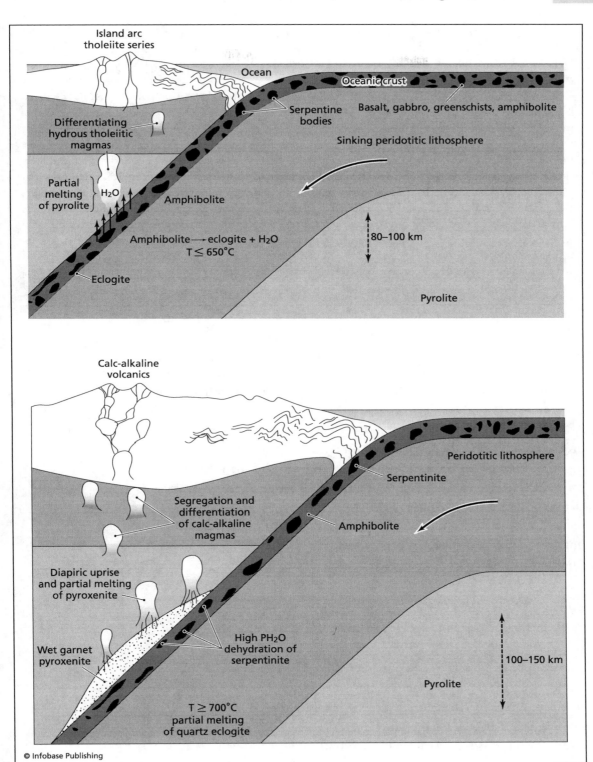

NORMAN LEVI BOWEN (1887–1956)

Dr. Norman Levi Bowen was one of the most brilliant igneous petrologists of the 20th century. Although he was born in Ontario, Canada, he spent most of his productive research career at the Geophysical Laboratories of the Carnegie Institute in Washington, D.C. Much of what is known about the sequence of melting of different minerals in rocks and the sequence in which they crystallize from magma was determined by Bowen. Bowen studied the relationships between plagioclase feldspars and iron-magnesium silicates in crystallizing and melting experiments. Based on these experiments, he derived the continuous and discontinuous reaction series explaining the sequence of crystallization and melting of these minerals in magmas. He also showed how magmatic differentiation by fractional crystallization can result from a granitic melt from an originally basaltic magma through the gradual crystallization of mafic minerals, leaving the felsic melt behind. Similarly, he showed how partial melting of one rock type can result in a melt with a different composition than the original rock, typically forming a more felsic melt than the original rock, and leaving a more mafic residue (or restite) behind.

Bowen also worked on reactions between rocks at high temperatures and pressures and the role of water in magmas. In 1928, he published his now-classic book *The Evolution of Igneous Rocks.*

solids (rocks). This process also results in the continuous change in the composition of the magma—if one mineral is removed the resulting composition is different. If some process removes these solidified crystals removed from the system of melts, a new magma composition results.

The removal of crystals from the melt system can occur by several processes, including the squeezing of melt away from the crystals or by sinking of dense crystals to the bottom of a magma chamber. These processes lead to magmatic differentiation by fractional crystallization, as first described by Norman Levi Bowen. Bowen systematically documented how crystallization of the first minerals changes the composition of the magma and results in the formation of progressively more silicic rocks with decreasing temperature.

Types of Volcanic Eruptions and Landforms

There is tremendous variety in the style of volcanic eruptions, both between volcanoes and from a single volcano during the course of an eruptive phase. This variety is related to the different types of magma produced by the different mechanisms previously described. Geologists have found it useful to classify volcanic eruptions based on how explosive the eruption may be, on which materials erupted, and by the type of landform produced by the volcanic eruption.

Tephra is material that comes out of a volcano during an eruption, and it may be thrown through the air or transported over land as part of a hot moving flow. Tephra includes both new magma from the volcano and older broken rock fragments that got caught in the eruption. It includes ash and *pyroclasts,* rocks ejected by the volcano. Large pyroclasts are called volcanic bombs; smaller fragments are lapilli; and the smallest grade into ash.

Hawaii Volcanoes National Park. Crater of Kilauea. Lava forms on the floor of the crater, near the trail from Volcano House of Halemaumau crater. The lava is typical pahoehoe. The smooth spot represents part of an earlier floor from 1902. *(USGS)*

While the most famous volcanic eruptions produce huge explosions, many eruptions are relatively quiet and nonexplosive. Nonexplosive eruptions have magma types that have low amounts of dissolved gases and tend to be basaltic in composition. Basalt flows easily and for long distances and tends not to have difficulty flowing out of volcanic necks. Nonexplosive eruptions may still be spectacular, as any visitor to Hawaii lucky enough to witness the fury of Pele, the Hawaiian goddess of the

Hawaii Volcanoes National Park. Eruption of Kilauea began in 1983. Fast-moving fluid `a`a breakout approaching Powerline Road at a 5,900- foot (1,798-m) elevation on the north side of flow 1B. Note a lava ball being rafted toward the flow front. Hank Moore at the left. 10:00 A.M., April 5, 1984 *(USGS)*

volcano, can testify. Mauna Loa, Kilauea, and other nonexplosive volcanoes produce a variety of eruption styles, including fast-moving flows and liquid rivers of lava, lava fountains that spew fingers of lava trailing streamers of light hundreds of feet into the air, and thick sticky lava flows that gradually creep downhill. The Hawaiians devised clever names for these flows, including `a`a for blocky rubble flows because walking across these flows in bare feet makes one exclaim "ah-ah" in pain. Pahoehoes are ropy-textured flows, after the Hawaiian term for rope.

Explosive volcanic eruptions are among the most dramatic natural events on Earth. With little warning, long-dormant volcanoes can explode with the force of hundreds of atomic bombs, pulverizing whole mountains and sending the existing material together with millions of tons of ash into the stratosphere. Explosive volcanic eruptions tend to be associated with volcanoes that produce andesitic or rhyolitic magma and have high contents of dissolved gases. These are mostly associated with convergent plate boundaries. Volcanoes that erupt magma with high contents of dissolved gases often produce a distinctive type of volcanic rock known as pumice, which resembles a sponge consisting of bubbles frozen in volcanic glass and minerals, in some cases light enough to float on water.

Mount Pinatubo, Philippines, June 1991. First major eruption of Mount Pinatubo, viewed from Clark Air Force Base. *(Karin Jackson, USGS)*

When the most explosive volcanoes erupt they produce huge eruption columns known as *Plinian* columns (named after Pliny the Elder, the Roman statesman, naturalist, and naval officer who died in 79 C.E. while struggling through thick ash while trying to rescue friends during the eruption of Mount Vesuvius). These eruption columns can reach 28 miles (45 km) in height and spew hot turbulent mixtures of ash, gas, and tephra into the atmosphere where winds may disperse them around the planet. Large ashfalls and tephra deposits may be spread across thousands of square miles. These explosive volcanoes also produce one of the scariest and most dangerous clouds on the planet. Nuée ardents are

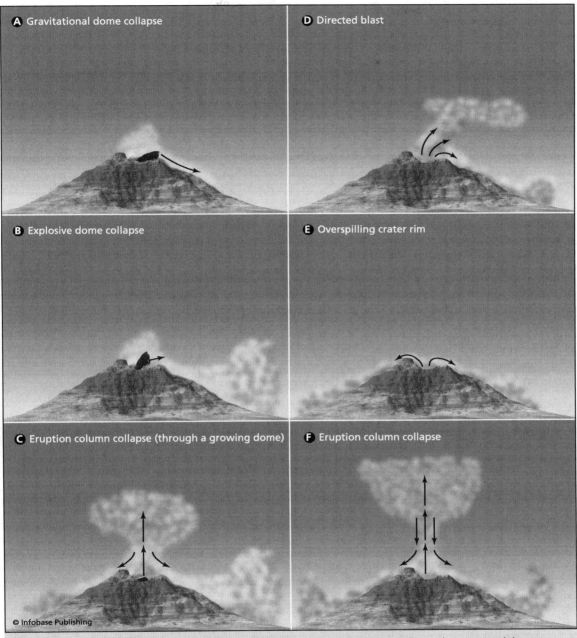

A Gravitational dome collapse

B Explosive dome collapse

C Eruption column collapse (through a growing dome)

D Directed blast

E Overspilling crater rim

F Eruption column collapse

© Infobase Publishing

Diagrams showing different types of eruptions that may form catastrophic pyroclastic flows. A) gravitational dome collapse; B) explosive dome collapse; C) eruption column collapse blasted through a growing dome; D) directed blast, with Mount Saint Helens being a recent example; E) eruption overspilling crater rim; F) eruption column collapse. If continuous, this produces large volume deposits, and, if discontinuous from discrete explosions, the deposits are smaller. *(Modified from A. L. Smith and M. J. Roobol)* hot glowing clouds of dense gas and ash that may reach temperatures of nearly 1,830°F (1,000°C) and rush down volcanic flanks at 450 MPH (700 km/h) and travel more than 60 miles (100 km) from the volcanic vent. Nuée ardents have been the nemesis of many a volcanologist and curious observer, as well as thousands upon thousands of unsuspecting or trusting villagers. Nuée ardents are but one type of pyroclastic flow, which includes a variety of mixtures of volcanic blocks, ash, gas, and lapilli that produce volcanic rocks called ignimbrites.

Most volcanic eruptions emanate from the central vents at the top of volcanic cones. However, many other flank eruptions have been recorded, where eruptions blast out of fissures on the side of the volcano. Occasionally, volcanoes blow out their sides, forming a lateral blast like the one that initiated the 1980 eruption of Mount Saint Helens in Washington State. This blast was so forceful that it began at the speed of sound, killing everything in the initial blast zone.

Volcanic landforms and landscapes are wonderful, dreadful, beautiful, and barren. They are as varied as the volcanic rocks and eruptions that produce them. Shield volcanoes include the largest and broadest mountains on the planet (Mauna Loa is more than 100 times as large as Mount Everest). These have slopes of only a few degrees, produced by basaltic lavas that flow long distances before cooling and solidifying. Stratovolcanoes, in contrast, are the familiar steep-sided cones like Mount Fuji, made of stickier lavas such as andesites and rhyolites, and they may have slopes of 30 degrees. Other volcanic constructs include cinder or tephra cones, including the San Francisco Peaks in Arizona, which are loose piles of cinder and tephra. Calderas, like Crater Lake in Oregon, are huge circular depressions, often many miles in diameter, that are produced when deep magma chambers under a volcano empty out (during an eruption). Such eruptions form huge empty spaces below the surface, and the overlying land collapses inward producing a topographic depression known as a caldera. Yellowstone Valley occupies one of the largest calderas in the United States. Many geysers, hot springs, and fumaroles in the valley are related to groundwater circulating to depths, being heated by shallow magma, and mixing with volcanic gases that escape through minor cracks in the crust of the Earth.

Volcanism in Relationship to Plate Tectonic Setting

The types of volcanism and associated volcanic hazards differ in various tectonic settings because each tectonic setting produces a different type of magma, through the processes described previously. Mid-ocean

Oblique aerial view of the eruption of May 18, 1980, which sent volcanic ash, steam, water, and debris to a height of 60,000 feet (18,288 m). The mountain lost 1,300 feet (396 m) of altitude and about 2/3 cubic mile (ca. 2.75 cubic km) of material. Note the material streaming downward from the center of the plume and the formation and movement of pyroclastic flows down the left flank of the volcano. *(Austin Post, USGS)*

ridges and intraplate *hot spot* types of volcanoes typically produce non-explosive eruptions, whereas convergent tectonic margin volcanoes may produce tremendously explosive and destructive eruptions. Much of the variability in the eruption style may be related to the different types of magma produced in these different settings and also to the amount of dissolved gases, or volatiles, in these magmas. Magmas with large amounts of volatiles tend to be highly explosive, whereas magmas with low contents of dissolved volatiles tend to be nonexplosive. The difference is very much like shaking two bottles, one containing soda and one containing water. The soda contains a high concentration of dissolved volatiles (carbon dioxide) and explodes when open. In contrast, the water has a low concentration of dissolved volatiles and does not explode when opened.

Eruptions from mid-ocean ridges are mainly basaltic flows, with low amounts of dissolved gases. These eruptions are relatively quiet, with basaltic magma flowing in underwater tubes and breaking off in bulbous shapes called *pillow lavas.* The eruption style in these underwater volcanoes is analogous to toothpaste being squeezed out of a tube. Eruptions from mid–ocean ridges may be observed in the few rare places where the ridges emerge above sea level, such as Iceland. Eruptions there include lava fountaining, where basaltic cinders are thrown a few hundred feet in the air and accumulate as cones of black glassy fragments, and long streamlike flows of basalt.

Hot spot volcanism tends to be much like that at mid-ocean ridges, particularly where the hot spots are located in the middle of oceanic plates. The Hawaiian Islands are home to the most famous hot spot volcanoes in the world, with the active volcanoes Kilauea and Mauna Loa on the island of Hawaii. Mauna Loa is a huge shield volcano, characterized by a very gentle slope of a few degrees from the base to the top. This gentle slope is produced by lava flows that have a very low viscosity (meaning they flow easily) and can flow and thin out over large distances before they solidify. Magmas with high viscosity would be much stickier and would solidify in short distances, producing volcanoes with steep slopes. Measured from its base on the Pacific Ocean seafloor to its summit, Mauna Loa is the tallest mountain in the world, a fact attributed to the large distances that its low-viscosity lavas flow and to the large volume of magma produced by this hot spot volcano.

Volcanoes associated with convergent plate boundaries produce by far the most violent and destructive eruptions. Recent convergent margin eruptions include Mount Saint Helens and two volcanoes in the

Philippines, Mount Pinatubo and Mayon volcano. The magmas from these volcanoes tend to be much more viscous, higher in silica content, and they have the highest concentration of dissolved gasses. Many of the dissolved gasses and volatiles, such as water, are released from the subducting oceanic plate as high mantle temperatures heat it up as it slides beneath the convergent margin volcanoes.

Conclusion

Plate tectonics and tectonic boundaries are extremely important for understanding volcanic hazards, since most of the planet's volcanic eruptions and many other geological hazards are located along and directly created by the interaction of plates. An understanding of plate tectonics is therefore essential for planning for geologic hazards and predicting the difference between eruption styles in various settings. Magma with different compositions, typically measured by variations in the abundance of silica, are found in various tectonic settings. Basaltic lava has silica contents of around 50 percent, andesitic lava of about 60 percent, and rhyolitic lavas near 70 percent. The subvolcanic equivalents of these rocks are known as gabbro, granodiorite, and granite. The relative ferocity of volcanic eruptions is related to silica content and to the amount of dissolved gases in the magma, with more dissolved gases producing more violent eruptions. Further variations are caused by differences in temperature, with higher temperature flows moving farther and faster than cooler magma.

Basaltic lavas with relatively quiet eruptions are found along extensional plate boundaries. However, most of the volcanism on the planet occurs along mid-ocean ridges, as the plates slowly move apart and magma upwells from the mantle to fill the space with basaltic magma that cools and solidifies to form new oceanic crust. Convergent plate boundaries may have extremely violent eruptions, forming fast-moving hot ash clouds, tall eruption columns, and suffocating blankets of ash that fall on surrounding communities. Volcanic eruptions sometimes happen in plate interiors, such as on the Hawaiian Islands. Most of these eruptions are basaltic in nature and relatively quiet. Occasionally, extremely large eruptions have occurred within plates, where hot spots are located in continents and large amounts of magma pooled within the crust before cataclysmic eruptions.

2

Volcanic Hazards

Volcanic eruptions have been responsible for the deaths of hundreds of thousands of people, and they directly affect large portions of the world's population, land-use patterns, and climate. The worst volcanic disasters have killed tens of thousands of people, whereas others may kill only a few thousand, hundreds, or even none. The following sections will demonstrate that specific phenomena associated with volcanic eruptions have been responsible for the greatest loss of life in individual eruptions. Understanding the specific hazards associated with volcanoes is important for reducing losses from future eruptions, especially considering that millions of people live close to active volcanoes. Some of the hazards are obvious, such as being overrun by lava flows, being buried by layers of ash, or being hit by hot glowing avalanche clouds known as nuée ardents. Other hazards are less obvious, such as poisonous gases that can seep out of volcanoes suffocating people nearby and changes to global climate as a consequence of large eruptions. The following table lists the 10 worst volcanic disasters in human history.

Hazards of Lava Flows

In some types of volcanic eruptions lava may bubble up or effuse from volcanic vents and cracks and flow like thick water across the land surface. During other eruptions lava oozes out more slowly, producing different types of flows with different hazards. Variations in magma composition, temperature, dissolved gas content, surface slope, and

The 10 Worst Volcanic Disasters in Human History		
VOLCANO, LOCATION	YEAR	NUMBER OF DEATHS
Tambora, Indonesia	1815	92,000
Krakatau, Indonesia	1883	36,500
Mount Peleé, Martinique	1902	29,000
Nevado del Ruiz, Colombia	1985	24,000
Santa Maria, Guatemala	1902	6,000
Galunggung, Indonesia	1822	5,500
Awu, Indonesia	1826	3,000
Lamington, Papua New Guinea	1951	2,950
Agung, Indonesia	1963	1,900
El Chichon, Mexico	1982	1,700

other factors lead to the formation of three major types of lava flow: `a`a, pahoehoe, and block lava. `A`a are characterized by rough surfaces of spiny and angular fragments, whereas pahoehoe have smooth ropy-like or billowing surfaces. Block lavas have larger fragments than `a`a flows and are typically formed by stickier, more silicic lavas. Some flows are transitional between these main types or may change from one type to another as surface slopes and flow rates change. It is common to see pahoehoe flows change into `a`a flows with increasing distance from the volcanic source.

Lava flows are most common around volcanoes that are characterized by eruptions of basalt, with low contents of dissolved gasses. About 90 percent of all lava flows worldwide are made of magma with basaltic composition, followed by andesitic (8 percent) and rhyolitic (2 percent). Places with abundant basaltic flows include Hawaii, Iceland, and other oceanic islands and mid-oceanic ridges, all characterized by nonexplosive eruptions. Virtually the entire Hawaiian chain is made of a series of lava flows piled high, one on top of the other. Most other volcanic islands are similar, including the Canary Islands in the Atlantic,

Réunion in the Indian Ocean, and the Galá-pagos Islands in the Pacific. In January 2002, massive lava flows erupted from Nyiragongo volcano in Congo, devastating the town of Goma and forcing 300,000 people to flee from their homes as the lava advanced through the town.

Lava flows generally follow topography, flowing from the volcanic vents downslope in valleys, much as streams of water from a flood would travel. Some lava flows may move as fast as water, up to almost 40 MPH (65 km/h), on steep slopes, but most move considerably slower. More typical rates of movement are about 10 feet (3 m) per hour to 10 feet (3 m) per day for slower flows. These rates of movement of lava allow most people to move out of danger to higher ground, but lava flows are responsible for significant amounts of property damage in places like Hawaii. Lava flows also are known to bury roads, farmlands, and other low-lying areas. It must be kept in mind, however, that the entire Hawaiian chain was built by lava flows and the land that is being damaged would not even be there if it were not for the lava flows. In general, pahoehoe flows flow the fastest, `a`a are intermediate, and block flows are the slowest.

This aerial photo shows the path of lava flows near a group of buildings in Goma, Congo, on Tuesday, January 22, 2002. About 90 percent of Goma's business district was consumed by lava when Mount Nyiragongo, 12 miles (20 km) north of lakeside Goma, erupted on January 17, sending huge lava flows through the city, cutting it in half. Most of the town has since been rebuilt on top of the new lava flows. *(Associated Press)*

Basaltic lava is extremely hot (typically about 1,900–2,100°F or 1,000°C–1,150°C) when it flows across the surface, so when it encounters buildings, trees, and other flammable objects they typically burst into flame and are destroyed. More silicic lavas may be slightly cooler, typically in the range of 1,550–1,920°F (850°–1,050°C). Most lavas will become semisolid and stop flowing at temperatures of around 1,380°F (750°C). Lavas typically cool quickly at first, until a crust or hard skin forms on the flow; then they cool much more slowly. One of the greatest hazards of lava flows is caused by this property of cooling. A lava flow may appear hard, cool, and safe to walk on, yet just below the thin surface may lie a thick layer of molten lava at temperatures of about 1,380°F (750°C). Many people have mistakenly thought it was safe to walk across a recent crusty lava flow, only to plunge through the crust to a fiery death. Thick flows may take years to crystallize and cool, and residents of some volcanic areas have learned to use the heat from flows for heating water and piping it to nearby towns.

It is significantly easier to avoid hazardous lava flows than some other volcanic hazards since in most cases it is possible to simply walk away from the hot moving lava. It is generally unwise to build or buy homes in low-lying areas adjacent to volcanoes, as these are the preferential sites for future lava flows to fill. Lava flows have been successfully diverted in a few examples in Hawaii, Iceland, and elsewhere. One of the better ways is to build large barriers of rock and soil to divert the flow from its natural course, to a place where it will not damage property. More creative methods have also had limited success: Lava flows have been bombed in Hawaii and Sicily, and spraying large amounts of water on active flows in Hawaii and Iceland has chilled these flows enough to stop their advance into harbors and populated areas.

Hazards of Pyroclastic Flows, Tephra Falls, and Ballistic Projectiles

While some volcanoes spew massive amounts of lava in relatively non-threatening flows, other volcanoes are extremely explosive and send huge eruption clouds tens of thousands of feet into the air. Violent pyroclastic flows present one of the most severe hazards associated with volcanism. Unlike slow-moving lava flows, pyroclastic flows may move at hundreds of miles per hour by riding on a cushion of air, burying entire villages or cities before anyone has a chance to escape. There are several varieties of pyroclastic flows and related volcanic emissions. Nuée ardents are particularly hazardous varieties of pyroclastic flows, with temperatures that may exceed 1,470°F (800°C), and downslope velocities measured in many hundreds of miles per hour. One of the most devastating pyroclastic flows of modern times was generated from a convergent margin arc volcano in the Lesser Antilles arc on the eastern edge of the Caribbean, between North and South America. On an otherwise quiet day in 1902, the city of Saint-Pierre on the beautiful Caribbean island of Martinique was quickly buried by a nuée ardent from Mount Pelée, killing more than 29,000 people. Pyroclastic surges are mixtures of gas and volcanic tephra that move sideways in a turbulent mixture that may flow over topography and fill in low-lying areas. A third type of pyroclastic flow is a lateral blast where an explosion removes large sections of a volcano and blows the material out sideways, typically with disastrous results. The May 1980 eruption of Mount Saint Helens was a laterally directed blast.

One of the most famous volcanic eruptions of all time was a pyroclastic flow. In 79 C.E., Mount Vesuvius of Italy erupted and buried the towns of Pompeii and Herculaneum under pyroclastic ash clouds, permanently encapsulating these cities and their inhabitants in volcanic ash. Later discovery and excavation of parts of these cities by archaeologists led to the world's better understanding of the horrors of being caught in a pyroclastic flow. People were found buried in ash, preserved in various poses of fear, suffocation, running, and attempts to shelter their children from the suffocating cloud of gas and ash. Crater Lake in Oregon provides a thought-provoking example of the volume of volcanic ash that may be produced during a pyroclastic eruption. The eruption that caused this caldera to collapse covered an area of 5,000 square miles (13,000 sq km) with more than 6 inches (15 cm) of ash and blanketed most of present-day Washington, Oregon, Idaho, and large parts of Montana, Nevada, British Columbia, and Alberta with ash. Larger eruptions have occurred: for instance, a thick rock unit known as the Bishop tuff (a term for hardened ash) covers a large part of the southwestern United States. If any of the active volcanoes in the western United States were to produce such an eruption, it would be devastating for the economy and huge numbers of lives would be lost.

Volcanoes spew a wide variety of sizes and shapes of hardened magma and wall rock fragments during eruptions. Tephra is a term that is used to describe all airborne products of an eruption except for gases. Volcanic ash and material erupted during pyroclastic flows may therefore be called tephra, as are other hard objects such as volcanic bombs, blocks, and lapilli. These terms describe material that is ejected out of the volcanic vent on ballis-

Image of pyroclastic flow rushing down Mount Unzen, Japan, with people running in foreground *(Associated Press)*

tic trajectories, potentially harming people and structures in their path or intended landing area. Volcanic bombs are clots of magma, more than 2.5 inches (6 cm) in diameter, ejected from a volcanic vent. Bombs have various shapes and sizes, with shape being determined by magma composition, gas content, and other factors. Volcanic blocks are pieces of the wall rock plucked from the walls of the vent and sent shooting through the air by the force of the eruption. These blocks tend to retain angular and blocky shapes. Lapilli are magma clots from ash-size to 2.5 inches (up to 6 cm) in diameter ejected from the volcano and are of many shapes and internal structure as well. Many lapilli form by rain drops moving through ash clouds, causing concentric layers of ash to build around the drop and fall to the ground.

During eruptions, projectiles may be thrown thousands of feet into the air and land thousands of feet from the volcanic vent. Some large volcanic bombs and blocks have been found at distances up to several miles from their sources. Most projectiles leave the volcanic vent at speeds of 300–2,000 feet per second (100–600 m/s) and land

Casts of humans buried in Pompeii by ash from eruption of Vesuvius *(Lee Bataglia, Photo Researchers, Inc.)*

on a near-vertical trajectory often forming impact craters where they land. It has been the misfortune of many volcano observers to be standing in the exact spot a volcanic bomb or block lands, with dire results. The volume of projectiles landing from a volcanic vent increases toward the vent, with steep-sided volcanoes often covered by fields of projectiles that land and then fragment and roll downhill.

During eruptions, large tephra clouds may explode upward and outward from the volcanic vent, expanding as the cloud incorporates more air as it rises. As it expands it becomes less dense, and the heavy particles in the clouds fall out covering the area below the cloud with blankets of tephra. The thickest tephra blankets are deposited closest to the volcano with the fallout pattern determined by the direction of the winds that carried the tephra cloud. Tephra blankets from major eruptions may cover hundreds of thousands of square miles with volcanic ash and tephra particles. Some of this may be so thick as to collapse buildings, suffocate plants, animals, and people, and sometimes may be hot enough to burn objects on impact. Tephra

Photo of volcanic bomb with breadcrust texture from Polovina Hill, Alaska *(G. S. Winer, Alaska Volcano Observatory)*

falls are associated with intense darkness for many hours or even days, with many historical accounts relating difficulty in seeing objects only inches from one's face. Some types of tephra are associated with high concentrations of poisonous sulfur compounds, leading to long-term crop and animal disease. Rains and wind quickly wash some tephra falls away. Other types of tephra blankets tend to form hard crusts or thick layers that solidify and become a new land surface in the affected areas.

Tephra falls tend to be hazardous for so many reasons, most relating to the size and physical characteristics of the ejecta. Eruption columns are typically 1.5–6 miles high (3–10 km) but may reach heights of more than 35 miles (55 km), covering huge areas downwind with thick layers of ash and tephra. Many falls occur rapidly, with downwind transport velocities of 5–60 MPH (10–100 km/hr). Ash from these clouds may be semitoxic, creating hazards for breathing and for vegetation. Additionally, ash is electrically conductive and magnetic when wet, causing problems for electronics and other infrastructure.

Hazards of Mudflows, Floods, Debris Flows, and Avalanches

When pyroclastic flows and nuée ardents move into large rivers, they quickly cool and mix with water, becoming fast-moving mudflows known as *lahars*. Lahars may also result from the extremely rapid melting of icecaps on volcanoes. A type of lahar in which ash, blocks of rock, trees, and other material are chaotically mixed together is known as a debris flow. Some lahars originate directly from a pyroclastic flow moving out of a volcano and into a river, whereas other lahars are secondary and form after the main eruption. These secondary, or rain-triggered lahars, form when rain soaks volcanic ash that typically covers a region after an eruption, causing the ash to be mobilized and flow downhill

Mount Pinatubo, Philippines. View of native house covered by ash on flanks of Pinatubo *(R. P. Hoblitt, USGS)*

Surge of floodwater coming down Smith Creek blast zone during first major rain after the May 18, 1980, eruption of Mount Saint Helens. *(Holly A. Martinson, USGS)*

into streams and rivers. It is estimated that it only takes about 30 percent water to mobilize an ash flow into a lahar. The hazards from lahars may continue for months or years after an ashfall on a volcano, as long as the ash remains in place and rains may come to remobilize the ash into flowing slurries. There is a gradual transition between pyroclastic flows, lahars, mud-laden river flows, and floods, with a progressively increasing water content and decreasing amount of suspended material. This transition generally takes place gradually as the flow moves away from the volcano. In other cases, earthquakes or the collapse of crater lakes may initiate lahars, such as occurred on Mount Pinatubo during its massive 1991 eruption. Jökulhlaups are massive floods produced by volcanic eruptions beneath glaciers and are common in Iceland where volcanoes of the mid-Atlantic ridge rise to the surface but are locally covered by glaciers. Other jökulhlaups are known to have originated beneath the snow-covered peaks of the high Andes Mountains in South America.

Lahars and mudflows were responsible for much of the burial of buildings and deaths from the trapping of automobiles during the 1980 eruption of Mount Saint Helens. Big river valleys were also filled by lahars and mudflows during the 1991 eruption of Mount Pinatubo in the Philippines, resulting in extensive property damage and loss of life. One of the greatest volcanic disasters of the 20th century resulted from the generation of a huge mudflow when the icecap on the volcano Nevado del Ruiz in Colombia catastrophically melted during the 1985 eruption. The water mixed with the volcanic ash on the slopes forming a wet slurry that was able to rapidly flow under the force of gravity. When the mudflow moved downhill it buried the towns along the rivers leading to the volcano, killing 23,000 people and causing more than U.S. $200 million of property damage.

Pyroclastic flows may leave thick unstable masses of unconsolidated volcanic ash that can be easily remobilized long after an eruption during heavy rains or earthquakes. These thick piles of ash may remain for many years after an eruption and not be remobilized until a hurricane or other heavy rainstorm (itself a catastrophe) fluidizes the ash, initiating destructive mudflows or other types of *mass washing* events.

The hazard potential from lahars depends on a wide range of their properties. The thicker and faster-moving lahars are the most danger-

Devastation along the South Fork Toutle River resulting from the May 18, 1980, lahars. Logs and other debris jammed up against the house. *(Lyn Topinka, USGS)*

Fumaroles at Spirit Lake, Mount Saint Helens, Washington, after the eruption in 1980. Steam rises almost constantly from these vents. *(USGS)*

ous and move the greatest distance from the volcanic source. In places where volcanoes have crater lakes the hazard potential from lahars and floods is directly proportional to the amount of water that is stored in the lake and may be catastrophically released. Thick piles of ash and tephra may be mobilized into lahars under different conditions, depending on the size of volcanic particles, thickness of the deposits, the angle of the slope they are deposited upon, and the amount of rain or snow that infiltrates the deposit. Communities located downhill (or down river valley) from volcanic slopes that are covered with ash need to make hazard assessments of the potential for remobilization of ash into lahars to protect citizens and property in low-lying areas.

Slope failures resulting from collapse of oversteepened volcanic constructs on volcanoes sometime produce debris avalanches and flows that can travel large distances in very short intervals of time. Globally there are more large debris avalanche catastrophes than there are caldera collapse events. Numerous successive debris avalanche deposits, suggesting that collapse of the slopes may be one of the most important processes that modify the slopes of volcanoes, flank many volcanoes. These deposits typically consist of unsorted masses of angular to subangular fragments with hummocky surfaces. Variations in the internal structure of the deposits depend on many factors such as the amount of air and water present in the mixture as it collapses. Water-rich debris avalanche deposits are transitional in nature with lahars. Some slope failures are associated with very dangerous lateral blasts of volcanoes, such as the 1980 eruption of Mount Saint Helens.

Hazards of Poisonous Gases

One of the lesser-known hazards of active volcanoes stems from their emission of gases. These gases normally escape through geysers, fumaroles, and fractures in the rock. In some instances, however, volcanoes emit poisonous gases, including carbon monoxide, carbon dioxide, and sulfurous gases. These may also mix with water to produce acidic pools of hydrochloric, hydrofluoric, and sulfuric acid. It is generally not advisable to swim in strange-colored or unusual smelling ponds on active volcanoes.

Some of the more devastating emissions of poisonous gases such as carbon dioxide from volcanoes occurred in 1984 and 1986 in Africa. In the larger of the emissions in 1986 approximately 1,700 people and thousands of cattle were killed when a huge cloud of invisible and odorless carbon dioxide bubbled out of Lakes Nyos and Monoun in volcanic craters in Cameroon, quickly suffocating the people and animals downwind from the vent lakes. More than 3.5 billion cubic feet (100 million cubic m) of gas emissions escaped without warning and spread out over the area in less than two hours, highlighting the dangers of living on and near active volcanoes. Lakes similar to Lakes Nyos and Monoun are found in many other active volcanic areas, including heavily populated parts of Japan, Zaire, and Indonesia.

Steps have recently been taken to reduce the hazards of additional gas emissions from these lakes. In 2001, a team of scientists from Cameroon, France, and the United States installed the first of a series of degassing pipes into the depths of Lake Nyos, in an attempt to release the gases from depths of the lake gradually, before they erupt catastrophically. The first pipe extends to 672 feet (205 m) deep in the lake and causes a pillar of gas-rich water to squirt up the pipe and form a fountain on the surface, slowly releasing the gas from depth. The scientific team estimates that they need five additional pipes to keep the gas levels at a safe level, which will cost an additional $2 million.

Hazards of Volcanic-Induced Earthquakes and Tsunamis

Minor earthquakes generally accompany volcanic eruptions. The typical scenes from old disaster movies where the ground shakes and the volcano erupts are actually not far from the true experience, though the earthquakes tend to be slightly exaggerated in the movies. The earthquakes are generated by magma forcing its way upward through cracks and fissures into the volcano from the magma chamber at depth. Gas explosions in the magma conduits under the volcano generate other earthquakes. The collapse of large blocks of rock into calderas or the shifting of mass in the volcano may also initiate earthquakes. Some of these earthquakes happen with regular frequency, or time between individual shocks, and are known as harmonic tremors. Harmonic tremors have been noted immediately before many volcanic eruptions. These earthquakes have therefore become one of the more reliable methods of predicting exactly when an eruption is imminent, as geologists can trace the movement of the magma by very detailed seismic monitoring. Harmonic tremor earthquakes typically form a continuous, low frequency rhythmic ground shaking that is distinct from the more isolated shocks associated with movement on faults. If you are near a volcano and feel these harmonic tremors, it is a good warning that it is time to leave. Some swarms of harmonic tremors precede an eruption by as little as a few hours or a day and other cases are reported where the harmonic tremors have gone on for a year before an eruption. Many volcanoes are located in tectonically active areas, and these regions also experience earthquakes that are related to plate movements instead of magma movement and impending volcanic eruptions. There is an ongoing debate in the scientific community about whether some earthquakes and plate movements have triggered magma migration and volcanic eruptions. For instance, the 1990 eruption of Mount Pinatubo in the Philippines was preceded by a large earthquake, but there is no direct evidence that the earthquake caused the eruption. It may, however, have opened cracks that allowed magma to rise to the surface, helping the eruption proceed.

Tsunamis, or giant seismic sea waves, may be generated by volcanic eruptions, particularly if the eruptions occur underwater. These giant waves may inundate coastlines with little warning and account for the greatest death toll for all volcanic hazards. For instance, in 1883 more than 36,000 people in Indonesia were killed by a tsunami generated by the eruption of Krakatau volcano. Most volcano-induced tsunamis are produced by the collapse of the upper part of the volcanic center into a caldera, displacing large amounts of water, which form a tsunami. Other volcanic tsunamis are induced by giant landslides, volcano-induced earthquakes, submarine explosions, and by pyroclastic material or lahars hitting sea water. Volcano-induced atmospheric shock waves may also initiate some tsunamis. The tsunami then moves radially away from the source at speeds of about 500 MPH (800 km/hr). The tsunami may have heights of a few feet at most in the open ocean and have wavelengths (distance between crests of successive waves) of 100 or more miles (~200 km). When the tsunami encounters and runs up onto shorelines, the shape of the seafloor, bays, promontories, and the coastline help determine the height of the wave (of course the initial height and distance also determine the height). Some bays that get progressively narrower tend to amplify the height of a tsunami, causing more destruction at their ends than at their mouths.

When tsunamis strike the coastal environment, the first effect is sometimes a significant retreat or drawdown of the water level; in other cases the water just starts to rise quickly. Since tsunamis have long wavelengths, it typically takes several minutes for the water to rise to its full height. Being that there is no trough right behind the crest of the wave, on account of the very long wavelength, the water does not recede for a considerable time after the initial crest rises onto land. The rate of rise of the water in a tsunami depends in part on the shape of the seafloor and the coastline. If the seafloor rises slowly, the tsunami may crest slowly, giving people time to outrun the rising water. In other cases, especially where the seafloor rises steeply, or the shape of the bay causes the wave to be amplified, the tsunami may come crashing in as huge walls of water with breaking waves that pummel the coast with a thundering roar and wreak utmost destruction.

Because tsunamis are waves, they travel in successive crests and troughs. Many deaths in tsunami events are related to people going to the shoreline to investigate the effects of the first wave or to rescue those injured or killed in the initial crest, only to be drowned or swept away in a succeeding crest. Tsunamis have long wavelengths, so there is a long lag time between individual crests. The period of a wave is the time between the passage of individual crests, and for tsunamis the period can be an hour or more. A tsunami may therefore devastate a shoreline area, retreat, and then another crest may strike an hour later, then another, and another in sequence.

Some of the largest recorded tsunamis have been generated by volcanic eruptions. The most famous volcanic eruption–induced tsunami included the series of huge waves generated by the eruption of Krakatau in 1883, which reached run-up heights of more than 200 feet (60 m) and killed 36,500 people. The number of people who perished in the eruption of Santorini in 1650 B.C.E. is not known, but the toll must have been huge. The waves reached 800 feet (240 m) in height on islands close to the volcanic vent of Santorini. Flood deposits have been found 300 feet (90 m) above sea level in parts of the Mediterranean Sea and extend as far as 200 miles (320 km) southward up the Nile River. Several geologists suggest that these were formed from a tsunami generated by the eruption of Santorini. The floods from this eruption may also, according to some scientists, account for the biblical parting of the Red Sea during the exodus of the Israelites from Egypt and the destruction of the Minoan civilization on the island of Crete.

Hazards of Atmospheric Sound and Shock Waves

Large volcanic eruptions are associated with rapid expansion of gases during explosive phases, and these have been known to produce some of the loudest sounds and atmospheric pressure waves known on Earth. For instance, explosions from the 1883 eruption of Krakatau were heard almost 3,000 miles (4,700 km) away, in places as diverse as the Indian Ocean islands of Diego Garcia and Rodriguez, in Southeast Asia across Myanmar, Thailand, and Vietnam, the Philippines, and across western

Tractors and trees blown over by the force of shock wave and hot ash cloud produced by the May 18, 1980, eruption of Mount Saint Helens. *(USGS)*

and central Australia. Other volcanic eruptions that produced blasts heard for hundreds to thousands of miles include the 1835 eruption of Cosigüina in Nicaragua, the eruption of Mount Pelée in 1902, and Mount Katmai in Alaska in 1912. Although interesting, sounds from eruptions are relatively harmless. Explosions that produce sound waves may also be associated with much more powerful atmospheric shock waves that can be destructive.

Atmospheric shock waves are produced by the pressure changes caused by the sudden explosive release of rapidly expanding steam and gases that may sometimes exceed the speed of sound. When the gas eruptions proceed at supersonic velocities (1,000–2,700 feet [305–823 m] per second depending on the temperature and density of the gas), the shock waves may be associated with huge, expanding flashing arcs of light that pulsate out of the volcano. Firsthand accounts of these flashing arcs are rare, but observations of the 1906 eruption of Vesuvius told of flashes ranging from several times a second to every few seconds. Deafening explosive sounds followed these flashes.

Large atmospheric shock waves may be powerful enough to damage or knock down buildings and may travel completely around the world. The eruptions of Krakatau in 1883, Pelée in 1902, and Asama (Japan) in 1783 and 1973, and others were recorded at atmospheric weather stations around the globe. Some of these shock waves destroyed or damaged buildings across hundreds of square miles around the volcano.

Many volcanic eruptions are associated with spectacular lightning storms in the ash clouds or in the expanding gas clouds. As this material is ejected from the volcano many particles may rub together creating electrical discharges seen as lightning. Intense lightning storms may extend typically for 5 to 10 miles (8–16 km) from the eruption, posing threats to people brave enough to remain close to the eruption and to communications systems. A phenomenon known as Saint Elmo's fire is sometimes associated with volcanic eruptions. It refers to a glowing blue or green electrical discharge that emanates from tall objects that are near an intense electrical charge and has been observed on ships near eruptions including Krakatau in 1883, Vesuvius in 1906, and the 1980 eruption of Mount Saint Helens.

Hazards from Changes in Climate

Some of the larger, more explosive volcanic eruptions spew vast amounts of ash and finer particles called aerosols into the atmosphere and stratosphere, and it can take years for these particles to settle back down to Earth. They get distributed about the planet by high-level winds, and they have the effect of blocking out some of the Sun's rays, which lowers global temperatures. This happens because particles and aerosol gases in the upper atmosphere tend to scatter sunlight back to space, lowering the amount of incoming solar energy. In contrast, particles that only get injected into the lower atmosphere absorb sunlight and contribute to greenhouse warming. A side effect is that the extra particles in the atmosphere also produce more spectacular sunsets and sunrises, as does extra pollution in the atmosphere. These effects were readily observed after the 1991 eruption of Mount Pinatubo, which spewed more than 172 billion cubic feet (5 billion cubic m) of ash and aerosols into the atmosphere, causing global cooling for two years after the eruption. Even more spectacularly, the 1815 eruption of Tambora in Indonesia caused three days of total darkness for approximately 300 miles (500 km) from the volcano, and it initiated the famous "year without a summer" in Europe, because the ash from this eruption lowered global temperatures by more than a degree. Even these amounts of gases and small airborne particles are dwarfed by the amount of material placed into the atmosphere during some of Earth's largest eruptions, known as flood basalts. No flood basalts have been formed on Earth for several tens of millions of years, which is a good thing, since their eruption may be associated with severe changes in climate. For instance, 66 million years ago a huge flood basalt field was erupted over parts of what is now western India, the Seychelles Island, and Madagascar. (These places were closer together then, but have since been separated by plate tectonics.) When the basalt field erupted, the climate changed drastically, and it is thought that these severe climate changes contributed to

GAIA HYPOTHESIS

At certain times in Earth's history, volcanism has been so intense and so much ash has been put in the atmosphere, little solar radiation could reach the surface. The planet should have become trapped in a runaway global icehouse, in which it was covered with ice, and from which it could not escape. For billions of years, Earth has maintained its temperature and atmospheric composition in a narrow range that has permitted life to exist on the surface, and the planet has always managed to escape from periods of deep-freeze and global warming. Many scientists have suggested that this remarkable trait of the planet is a result of life adapting to conditions that happen to exist and evolving on the planet. An alternative idea has emerged that the planet behaves as some kind of self-regulating organism that invokes a series of positive and negative feedback mechanisms to maintain conditions within the narrow window in which life can exist. In this scenario, organisms and their environment evolve together as a single coupled system, regulating the atmospheric chemistry and composition to the need of the system. This second idea, known as the Gaia hypothesis, was pioneered by Dr. James Lovelock, an atmospheric chemist at Green College in Oxford, England. However, the idea of a living planet dates back at least to Sir Issac Newton.

How does the Gaia hypothesis work? The atmosphere is chemically unstable, yet has maintained conditions conducive for life for billions of years despite a 30 percent increase in solar luminosity since the Early Precambrian. The basic tenet of the hypothesis is that organisms, particularly microorganisms, are able to regulate the atmospheric chemistry and hence temperature to keep conditions suitable for their development. Although widely criticized, some of the regulating mechanisms have been found to exist, lending credence to the possibility that Gaia may work. Biogeochemical cycles of nutrients including iodine and sulfur have been identified, with increases in the nutrient supply from land to ocean leading to increased biological production and increased emissions to the atmosphere. Increased production decreases the flux of nutrients from the oceans to the land, in turn decreasing the nutrient supply and decreasing biological production and emissions to the atmosphere.

As climate warms, rainfall increases and the weathering of calcium-silicate rocks increases. The free calcium ions released during weathering combine with atmospheric carbon dioxide to produce

(continues)

(continued)

carbonate sediments, effectively removing the greenhouse gas carbon dioxide from the atmosphere. This reduces global temperatures in another self-regulating process. An additional feedback mechanism was discovered between ocean algae and climate. Ocean algae produce dimethyl sulfide gas, which oxidizes in the atmosphere to produce nucleii for cloud condensation. The more dimethyl sulfide that algae produce, the more clouds form, lowering temperatures and lowering algal production of dimethyl sulfide in a self-regulating process.

That the Earth and its organisms have maintained conditions conducive for life for four billion years is clear. However, at times the Earth has experienced global icehouse and global hothouse conditions, where conditions extend beyond the normal range. Lovelock relates these brief intervals of Earth history to fevers in an organism and notes that the planet has always recovered. Life has evolved dramatically on Earth in the past four billion years, but this is compatible with Gaia. Living organisms can both evolve with and adapt to their environment, responding to changing climates by regulating or buffering changes to keep conditions within limits that are tolerable to life on the planet as a whole. However, there are certainly limits, and the planet has never experienced organisms such as humans that continually emit huge quantities of harmful industrial gases to the atmosphere. It is possible that the planet, or Gaia, will respond by making conditions on Earth uninhabitable for humans, saving the other species on the planet. As time goes on, in about a billion years, the Sun will expand and eventually burn all the water and atmosphere off the planet, making it virtually uninhabitable. By then humans will hopefully have solved the problem of where to move to and have developed the means to move global populations to a new planet.

massive global extinction of most living things on Earth at the time, including the dinosaurs. The atmospheric changes stressed the global environment to such an extent that when another catastrophic event, a meteorite impact, occurred, the additional environmental stresses caused by the impact were too great for most life to handle.

Aside from global cooling or warming associated with major volcanic eruptions, volcanic gases and ash can have some severe effects on regional environmental conditions. Gases and aerosols (fine particles suspended in gas) may be acidic and carried far from the source as gases, aerosols, salts, or adsorbed on the ash and tephra particles. Some of these compounds, including sulfur and chlorine are acidic and may mix with water and other cations to form sulfuric and sulfurous acids, as well as hydrochloric acid, hydrofluoric acid, carbonic acid, and ammonia. Ashfalls and rains that move through ash clouds and deposits may spread harmful and acidic fluids that can have harmful effects on vegetation, crops, and water supplies. Other volcanic eruptions have been associated with more toxic gases, such as concentrated fluorine, which has occasionally posed a hazard in Iceland.

Other Hazards and Long-Term Effects of Volcanic Eruptions

Dispersed ash may leave thin layers on agricultural fields, which may be beneficial or detrimental, depending on the composition of the ash. Much of the richest farmland on the planet is on volcanic ash layers near volcanoes. Some ash basically fertilizes soil, whereas other ash is toxic to livestock. Volcanic ash consists of tiny but jagged and rough particles that may conduct electricity when wet. These properties make ash pose severe hazards to electronics and machinery that may last many months past an eruption. In this way ash has been known to disrupt power generation and telecommunications. The particles are abrasive and, if inhaled, may cause serious heart and lung ailments.

Ash clouds have some unexpected and long-term consequences to the planet and its inhabitants. Airplane pilots have sometimes mistakenly flown into ash clouds, thinking they are normal clouds, which has caused engines to fail. For instance, KLM flight 867 with 231 people aboard flew through the ash cloud produced during the 1989 eruption of Mount Redoubt in Alaska, causing engine failure. The plane suddenly dropped two miles (3.2 km) in altitude before the pilots were able to restart the engines, narrowly averting disaster. This event led the United States Geological Survey (USGS) to formulate a series of warning codes for eruptions in Alaska and their level of danger to aircraft.

After volcanic eruptions, large populations of people may be displaced from their homes and livelihoods for extended or permanent time periods. In many cases these people are placed in temporary refugee camps, which all too often become permanent shanty villages, riddled with disease, poverty, and famine. Many of the casualties from volcanic eruptions come from these long-term effects and not the initial eruption. More needs to be done to ensure that populations displaced by volcanic disasters are relocated into safe settings.

Conclusion

Volcanic eruptions are associated with a specific suite of hazards that account for most fatalities and damage during eruptions. Understanding the threat posed by each of these hazards can potentially save lives and reduce property loss during eruption events. The movement of lava flows generally poses the least threat to life, since they generally move slowly, yet flows may not be stopped before they consume buildings or villages in their paths. In contrast, pyroclastic flows can move at hundreds of miles per hour, overwhelming, burning, and burying all in their path. Volcanic ash deposited on volcanic slopes can become unstable for years after eruptions when the ash becomes saturated with water and then moves downslope as a thick ash-water mixture known as a lahar, that may harden to a cementlike texture upon drying. Lahars have buried many villages and killed thousands of people in the past century. Some volcanoes emit poisonous gases, which can be fatal to humans and livestock. Some lakes on volcanoes have suddenly released huge volumes of carbon dioxide gas, which has moved downhill suffocating thousands of people and animals. Volcanic eruptions may also generate earthquakes and tsunamis, causing damage from the shaking and run-up of the waves in coastal regions. Large volumes of gas emitted from volcanoes can change global temperatures, typically lowering temperatures by about a degree for a year or two. Large flood-basalt volcanism has the potential to change global climates for extended periods of geological time.

3

Reducing the Threat from Volcanic Hazards

One of the best ways to understand what to anticipate from an active volcano is to study its history. Historical records can be examined to learn about recent eruptions. Geological mapping and analysis can reveal what types of material the volcano has spewed forth in the more distant past. A geologist who studies volcanic deposits can tell through examination of these deposits whether the volcano is characterized by explosive or nonexplosive eruptions, whether it has nuée ardents or mudflows, and how frequently it has erupted over long intervals of time. This type of information is crucial for estimating what the risks are for any individual volcano. Programs of risk assessment and volcanic risk mapping need to be done around all of the nearly 600 active volcanoes of the world. These risk assessments will determine which areas are prone to ashfalls and which have been repeatedly hit by mudflows. They will help residents determine if there are any areas characterized by periodic emissions of poisonous gas. Approximately 60 eruptions occur globally every year, so the data would prove immediately useful when eruptions appear imminent.

Predicting Volcanic Eruptions
VOLCANIC ERUPTION STATISTICS

Nearly a quarter million people have died in volcanic eruptions in the past 400 years, with a couple of dozen volcanic eruptions killing more than 1,000 people each. Eruptions in remote areas have little consequence except for global climate change. In contrast, eruptions in populated areas can cause billions of dollars in damage and result in entire towns and cities being relocated. The eruption of Mount Saint Helens in 1980 did $1 billion worth of damage, and this was not even a very catastrophic eruption in terms of the volume of material emitted. The Mount Saint Helens eruption spewed about one cubic mile (4 cubic km) of material into the atmosphere, whereas 10 years later the eruption of Mount Pinatubo in the Philippines sent five–six cubic miles (20–25 cubic km) of material skyward. The table below lists a selection of the deadliest volcanic eruptions.

The USGS is the main organization in charge of monitoring volcanoes and eruptions in the United States and takes this responsibility for many other places around the world. In cases of severe eruptions or eruptions that threaten populated areas, other agencies such as the Federal Emergency Management Agency (FEMA) will join the USGS and help in disseminating information and evacuating the population.

Sixteen Deadly Volcanic Eruptions		
LOCATION	YEAR	DEATHS
Tambora, Indonesia	1815	92,000
Krakatau, Indonesia	1883	36,500
Mount Pelée, Martinique	1902	32,000
Nevado del Ruiz, Colombia	1985	24,000
Unzen, Japan	1792	14,300
Laki, Iceland	1783	9,350
Kelut, Indonesia	1919	5,110
Santa Maria, Guatemala	1902	6,000
Galunggung, Indonesia	1822	5,500
Vesuvius, Italy	1631	3,500
Vesuvius, Italy	79	3,360
Awu, Indonesia	1826	3,000

LOCATION	YEAR	DEATHS
Papandayan, Indonesia	1772	2,957
Lamington, Papua New Guinea	1951	2,950
El Chichon, Mexico	1982	2,000
Agung, Indonesia	1963	1,900
Sofriere, St. Vincent	1902	1,680
Oshima, Japan	1741	1,475
Asama, Japan	1783	1,377
Taal, Philippines	1911	1,335
Mayon, Philippines	1814	1,200
Agung, Indonesia	1963	1,184
Cotopaxi, Ecuador	1877	1,000
Pinatubo, Philippines	1991	800

PRECURSORS TO ERUPTIONS

Volcanic eruptions are sometimes preceded by a number of precursory phenomena, or warnings that an eruption may be imminent. Many of these involve subtle changes in the shape or other physical characteristics of the volcano. Many volcanoes develop bulges, swells, or domes on their flanks when magma rises before an eruption. These shape changes can be measured using sensitive devices called tilt meters, that measure tilting of the ground surfaces, or other devices that precisely measure distances between points, such as geodolites and laser measuring devices. Bulges were measured on the flanks of Mount Saint Helens before the 1980 eruption.

Eruptions may also be preceded by other more subtle events, such as increase in the temperature or heat flow from the volcano, measurable both on the surface and in crater lakes, hot springs, fumaroles, and hot springs on the volcano. There may also be detectable changes in the composition of gases emitted by the volcano, such as increases in the hydrochloric acid and sulfur dioxide gases before an eruption.

One of the most reliable precursors to an eruption is the initiation of the harmonic seismic tremors that reflect the movement of magma into the volcano. These tremors typically begin days or weeks before an eruption and steadily change their characteristics, enabling successively more accurate predictions of how imminent the eruption is before it actually happens. Careful analysis of precursor phenomena including the harmonic tremors, change in the shape of the volcano, and emission of gases has enabled accurate prediction of volcanic eruptions, including Mount Saint Helens and Mount Pinatubo. These predictions saved innumerable lives.

VOLCANO MONITORING

Signs that a volcano may be about to erupt may only be observed if volcanoes are carefully and routinely monitored. Volcanic monitoring is aimed at detecting the precursory phenomena described above and tracking the movement of magma beneath volcanoes. In the United States, the USGS is in charge of comprehensive volcano monitoring programs in the Pacific Northwest, Alaska, and Hawaii.

One of the most accurate methods of determining the position and movement of magma in volcanoes is using seismology, or the study of the passage of seismic waves through the volcano. Seismic waves that travel through the Earth are known as *body waves.* These can be natural seismic waves generated by earthquakes beneath the volcano or seismic energy released by geologists who set off explosions and monitor how the energy propagates through the volcano. Certain types of body waves travel through fluids like magma (*compressional waves,* or P-waves), whereas other types of seismic waves do not (*shear waves,* or S-waves). The position of the magma beneath a volcano can be determined by detonating an explosion on one side of the volcano and having seismic receivers placed around the volcano to determine the position of a shadow zone where P-waves are received, but S-waves are not. The body of magma that creates the shadow zone can be mapped out in three dimensions by using data from the numerous seismic receiver stations. Repeated experiments over time can track the movement of the magma.

Other precursory phenomena are also monitored to track their changes with time, which can further refine estimates of impending eruptions. Changes in the temperature of the surface can be monitored by thermal infrared satellite imagery, and other changes, such as shifts in the composition of emitted gases, are monitored. Other promising precursors may be found in changes to physical properties, such as the electrical and magnetic field around volcanoes prior to eruptions.

Changes in the geochemical nature of gases and fluids coming out of volcanic vents and fumaroles can be used as indicators of activity beneath volcanoes. These changes depend largely on the changing rates of magma degassing beneath the volcano and interactions of the magma with the groundwater system. Monitoring of gases are designed to look largely for rapid changes or nonequilibrium conditions in hydrochloric and sulfurous acids, carbonic acids, oxygen, nitrogen, and hydrogen sulfide. Convergent margin andesitic types of explosive volcanoes show the greatest variation in composition of gases prior to eruption, since magma in these volcanoes is ultimately derived from fluids carried to depth by the subducting oceanic lithospheric slabs.

The details of geophysical volcano monitoring are complex and have undergone a rapid explosion in sophistication in recent years. One of the more common techniques in use now involves the use of a dense array or group of very sensitive *seismographs* called broadband seismometers that can detect a variety of earthquakes. Broadband seismometers can detect seismic waves with frequencies of 0.1–100 seconds, a great improvement over earlier short-period seismometers that only detected frequencies between 0.1–1 second. Swarms of small earthquakes, known as harmonic tremors, are sometimes associated with the movement of magma upward or laterally beneath a volcano, and they characteristically increase in number before an eruption. These are different from tectonic earthquakes that generally follow a pattern of main shock-aftershocks. By analysis of the seismic data from the array of seismographs, geologists are able to build a three-dimensional image of the area beneath the volcano, much like a tomographic image or a CAT scan, and thereby monitor the distribution and movement of magma beneath the volcano. When the magma gets closer to the surface an eruption is more likely to occur. Movement of magma is also sometimes associated with explosion-type earthquakes, easily differentiated from earthquakes associated with movement on faults.

Many explosive volcanic eruptions are preceded by swelling, bulging, or other deformation of the ground surface on the volcano, so one method to predict eruptions involves measuring and monitoring this bulging. Ground deformation is commonly measured using a variety of devices. Some instruments precisely measure shifts in the level surface, others measure tilting, and still others make electronic distance measurements. These types of measurements have recently increased

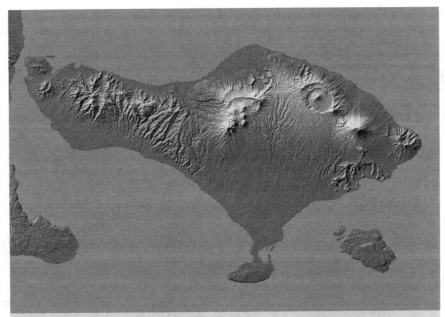

Shaded relief map of Bali Island in Indonesia showing volcanic cones and large circular caldera depressions *(NASA)*

in accuracy with the advent of the use of precise global positioning system (gps) instruments that allow measurements of latitude, longitude, and elevation to be made that are accurate to less than 0.5 inch (1 cm) even in very remote locations.

Observations have been made of phenomena that precede some eruptions, even though their cause is not clearly understood. Electrical and magnetic fields have been observed to show changes at many volcanoes, especially those with basaltic magma that has a high concentration of magnetic minerals. These changes may be related to movement of magma (and the magnetic minerals), changes in heating, movement of gases, or other causes. Recent studies have been able to link small changes in the microgravity fields around active volcanoes, especially explosive andesitic volcanoes, to movement of magma beneath the cones.

Satellite images are now commonly used to map volcanic deposits and features and to monitor eruptions. There is now a wide range of features satellites can measure and monitor, including large parts of the electromagnetic spectrum. Changes in the volcanic surface, growth of domes, and opening and closing of fissures on the volcano can be observed from satellites. Some satellites use radar technology that is able to see through clouds and some ash and, thus, are particularly

Photo of eruption plume from Augustine volcano in Alaska that was monitored from space satellites
(Game McGimsey, Alaska Volcano Observatory, USGS)

helpful for monitoring volcanoes in remote areas, in bad weather, at night, and during eruptions. A technique called radar interferometry can measure ground deformation at the sub-inch scale, showing bulges and swelling related to buildup of magma beneath the volcano. Some satellites can measure and monitor the temperature of the surface, and others can watch eruption plumes, ash clouds, and other atmospheric effects on a global scale.

Together all these techniques have given seismologists and geologists tools they need to make more accurate predictions of when an eruption may occur, saving lives and property. When many of the techniques are integrated in one monitoring program then scientists are better able to predict when the next eruption may occur. Several volcano monitoring programs in the United States use many different types of observations to provide for the safety of citizens. These include the Alaskan Volcano Observatory, the Cascades Volcano Observatory, and the Hawaii Volcano Observatory.

VOLCANO MONITORING AT
THE ALASKA VOLCANO OBSERVATORY

The Alaska Volcano Observatory is a joint program of the USGS, the Geophysical Institute of the University of Alaska Fairbanks, and the State of Alaska Division of Geological and Geophysical Surveys. The observatory was formed in 1988 and uses federal, state, and university resources to monitor and study Alaska's hazardous volcanoes, to predict and record eruptive activity, and to mitigate volcanic hazards to life and property.

Geologists affiliated with the Alaska Volcano Observatory perform the following three main tasks:

· They conduct monitoring and other scientific investigations in order to assess the nature, timing, and likelihood of volcanic activity;
· They assess volcanic hazards associated with anticipated activity, including kinds of events, their effects, and areas at risk;
· They provide timely and accurate information on volcanic hazards, and warnings of impending dangerous activity, to local, state, and federal officials and the public.

The backbone of the Alaska Volcano Observatory's volcano monitoring program consists of networks of continuously recording seismometers installed at selected volcanoes. Seismic data are relayed to facilities in Fairbanks and Anchorage where they are analyzed both automatically and by analysts. Initially, observatory staff concentrated their monitoring efforts on the four Cook Inlet volcanoes because they are closest to Alaska population centers. In response to the increasing hazard to aviation from volcanic ash, an expansion program was started in 1996 to include other volcanoes in the Aleutian Islands and on the Alaska Peninsula and now monitors more than 20 volcanoes. Volcanic unrest, caused by the migration of magma and other fluids through Earth's crust, is heralded by increased seismicity, often months to weeks before eruption. Because the seismometers provide a continuous data stream the onset of explosive eruptions can be detected quickly in most cases and appropriate warnings issued. An electronic alarm system is employed during nonbusiness hours.

Satellite imagery provides information that complements seismic monitoring at those volcanoes with seismic networks and is the only source of routine monitoring information at those without. The Alaska Volcano Observatory analyzes available satellite data twice daily for thermal anomalies and ash plumes at about 80 volcanoes in the north Pacific. Thermal anomalies at volcanic vents have been detected up to several weeks before large eruptions. Volcanic ash erupted into the atmosphere is a serious hazard to jet aircraft because it can cause their engines to shut down as it is ingested. By analyzing satellite imagery and working with the National Weather Service to predict where winds will carry the ash, the observatory assists the Federal Aviation Administration in warning aircraft of areas to avoid.

Space-based deformation monitoring is an emerging technique. The Alaska Volcano Observatory operates a network of precise Global Positioning System (GPS) receivers at Augustine Volcano in lower Cook Inlet that provide a continuous record of ground deformation. The observatory also conducts periodic field-based GPS surveys, as well as measures deformation with satellite radar interferometry (InSAR) techniques. These techniques are providing important information about inflation and deflation of volcanoes, but are not yet evolved enough for routine real-time monitoring of many volcanoes.

Experiencing a Volcanic Eruption

The wide variety of eruption types described here has shown that any response to an eruption will depend on what kind of eruption is being experienced. Anyone finding themselves near an impending explosive eruption, after eruption warnings have been issued, should try to evacuate the area as quickly as possible. Avoid low-lying areas that may be prone to mudslides, lahars, or debris avalanches, and especially steer clear of possible routes of hot glowing avalanches. It is advisable to travel far from the volcano before it erupts since travel routes may become crowded or jammed after the eruption occurs. Residents who live near or frequently visit areas near active volcanoes should make themselves aware of areas where these hazards are particularly high. Information on hazards of specific volcanoes is available from the USGS and local government offices. Some useful Web sites for U.S. volcanoes are listed in the bibliography.

Even the relatively passive eruptions of Hawaii pose many risks and hazards to those who view eruptions. Specific hazards include collapse of lava benches, especially where lava flows meet the sea, and on lava tubes. It is not uncommon for large benches of recently formed lava in Hawaii to suddenly collapse into the sea, setting off a series of explosions and sending waves of scalding hot water onto the land. Tephra jets are hazardous explosions of lava and steam formed where waves from the ocean splash against lava pouring into the sea. Sometimes these explosions can send volcanic bombs that are as large as a person many tens of feet through the air, so it is best to stay at least a few hundred feet from where lava is entering the sea. Lava can also make lava haze and volcanic smog that can contain poisonous and irritating sulfur dioxide and other hazardous gases, and also severely limit visibility. It is best to stay away from suspicious white clouds near active lava flows.

Conclusion

Volcanic eruptions have killed hundreds of thousands of people over the past few hundreds of years and displaced or affected tens of millions more people. Reducing the threat from volcanic eruptions depends on understanding the specific hazards associated with each volcano or volcanic province. Mapping the history of the style of eruptions from a specific volcano can help predict how the volcano may behave during future eruptions. Volcanoes that have a history of minor nonexplosive eruptions are likely to remain relatively nonthreatening, whereas volcanoes that have produced major ash clouds, mudflows, and explosive eruptions are likely to do so again. Volcano monitoring programs are able to use a combination of satellite-based monitoring, ground geophysical observations including local seismic networks, and monitors of temperature, bulging, and gas emissions on the volcano to monitor changes that could indicate when an eruption is imminent. Volcanoes that are particularly threatening to populated areas should be monitored most closely, with local volcano observatories that study the threats from the volcano, educate the public about how to respond in the event of an emergency, and set up a sequential series of threat level warnings that the public can respond to in the event of a volcanic emergency. Any individual's experience during a volcanic eruption will depend on how well the behavior of the volcano is predicted and how well the escape routes and emergency plans have been implemented.

4

Examples of Historical Volcanic Disasters

Much can be learned about volcanic hazards through an examination of historical eruptions. In this chapter, some of history's greatest eruptions that occurred before 1900 are examined, looking at the volcanic features that were most deadly and how they affected the populations. Examination of historical eruptions also provides a perspective where short-term, medium-term, and long-term effects of the eruption on populations can be examined. In some cases, regions recovered relatively quickly from large eruptions, whereas in other cases entire civilizations were destroyed.

Thera, Greece, 3,650 Years before Present

One of the greatest volcanic eruptions in the history of the human race happened approximately 3,650 years ago in the eastern Mediterranean region, then the cradle of civilization. Santorini is a small, elliptically shaped archipelago approximately 10 miles (16 km) across, located about 70 miles (110 km) north of the island of Crete. These islands are dark and ominous in stark contrast to Greece's other white limestone islands, and they form ragged, 1,300-foot (390-m) peaks that seem to point up toward something that should be in the center of the ring-shaped archipelago, but is no longer there. The peaks are pointing in toward the center of a giant caldera complex that erupted in the late Bronze Age, approximately 3,650 years ago, devastating much of the eastern Mediterranean. The largest island on the rim of the caldera is

Thera and across two circular 900–1,000-foot- (275–300-m-) deep calderas rests the opposing island of Therasia, once part of the same volcano. In the center of the composite caldera complex are several smaller islands known as the Kameni Islands, which represent newer volcanic cones growing out of the old caldera.

Santorini and Thera are part of the Cyclades Islands that form part of the Hellenic volcanic arc that stretches from western Turkey through Greece, lying above a subduction zone in the Mediterranean along which part of the African plate is being pushed beneath Europe and Asia. Volcanoes in the Hellenic arc are widely spaced, and numerous earthquakes also characterize the region. The area was apparently densely populated, as remnants of Bronze Age and earlier Neolithic settlements and villages along the coastal Aegean are buried in ash from Thera. Settlers who arrived about 6,000–7,000 years ago and traded with Crete and Greece populated the island of Thera. In 1967, archaeologists discovered a Bronze Age city buried by ash from the eruption and uncovered numerous paved streets and frescos, estimating that the city was at least the size of Pompeii when it was buried by the eruption of Vesuvius more than 1,700 years later. At the time of the eruption in Thera, the region was dominated by the Minoan culture, derived from Crete. The eruption occurred while a primitive form of writing was used by the Minoans, which has not been deciphered, and the Greek language had not yet been codified in writing. Thus, no local recorded texts record the eruption, although Hebrew text was in use in nearby Egypt and Israel. Some scholars have tried to link the eruption of Thera with biblical events such as the plagues, days of darkness, and parting of the Red Sea during the exodus of the Israelites from Egypt, although the timing of the eruption seems to be off by a couple of centuries for such a correlation to be made. The best current estimates for the age of the eruption are between 1690–1620 B.C.E.

Before the cataclysmic eruption, the Santorini Islands were one giant volcano known to the Greeks as Stronghyle, or the round one, and now referred to as Thera. We have no written firsthand accounts of the eruption of Thera, so the history has been established by geological mapping

(opposite page) (a) Map of the eastern Mediterranean showing the tectonic setting of Thera in the Hellenic volcanic arc. Note how Thera is located along a major fault above a subduction zone. (b) Detailed map of Santorini archipelago, showing modern Thera surrounding the large calderas that collapsed 3,650 years ago. *(Modified after J. de Boer and D. Sanders)*

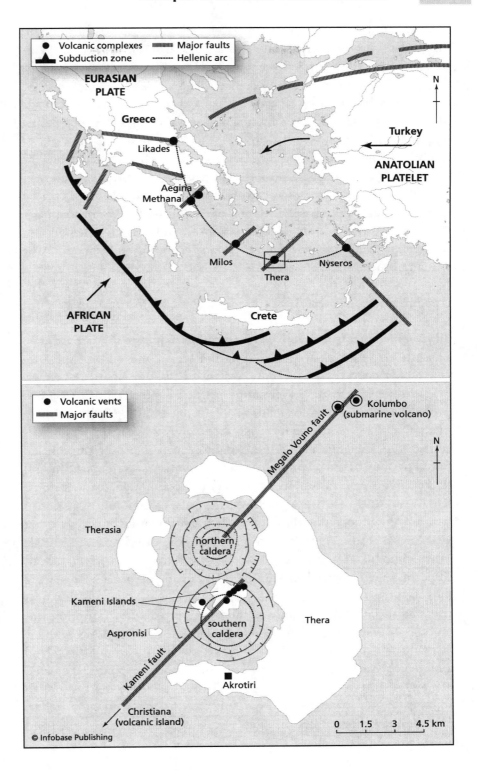

© Infobase Publishing

and examination of historical and archaeological records of devastation across the Mediterranean region. Volcanism on the island seems to have started 1–2 million years ago and continues to this day. Large eruptions are known to have occurred from 100,000, 80,000, 54,000, 37,000, and 16,000 years ago; then, finally, 3,650 years ago. The inside of Thera's caldera is marked by striking layers of black lava alternating with red and white ash layers, capped by a 200-foot- (60-m-) thick layer of pink to white ash and pumice that represents the deposits from the cataclysmic Bronze Age eruption. Ash from the eruption spread over the entire eastern Mediterranean and also on North Africa and across much of the Middle East. The most violent eruptions are thought to have occurred when the calderas collapsed and seawater rushed into the crater, forming a tremendous steam eruption and tsunami. The tsunami moved quickly across the Mediterranean, devastating coastal communities in Crete, Greece, Turkey, North Africa, and Israel. The tsunami was so powerful that it caused the Nile to run backward for hundreds of miles.

Detailed reconstructions of the eruption sequence reveal four main phases. The first was a massive eruption of ash and pumice that was ejected high into the atmosphere, collapsing back on Thera and covering nearby oceans with 20 feet of pyroclastic deposits. This phase was probably a Plinian eruption column and its devastating effects on Thera made the island uninhabitable. (Approximately 20 years passed before some settlers tried to reinhabit the island.) Huge fissures in the volcano began to open in the second phase, and seawater entered these and initiated large steam eruptions and mudflows, leaving deposits up to 65 feet (20 m) thick. The third phase was the most cataclysmic, as seawater began to enter deep into the magma chamber initiating huge blasts that were heard across southern Europe, northern Africa, and the Middle East. Sonic blasts and pressure waves would have been felt for thousands of miles around. Huge amounts of ash and aerosols were ejected into the atmosphere, probably causing several days of virtual darkness over the eastern Mediterranean. The fourth phase of the eruption was marked by continued production of pyroclastic flows depositing many layers of ash, pumice, and other pyroclastic deposits around the island and nearby Aegean. Most estimates of the amount of material ejected during the eruption fall around 20 cubic miles (80 cubic km), although some estimates are twice that amount. Ash layers from the eruption of Thera have been found in Egypt, Turkey, other Greek Islands, and across the Middle East.

Thera undoubtedly caused global atmospheric changes after ejecting so much material into the upper atmosphere. Data from Greenland ice cores indicate that a major volcanic eruption lowered Northern Hemisphere temperatures by ejecting aerosols and sulfuric acid droplets into the atmosphere in 1645 B.C.E. Additional evidence of an atmospheric cooling event caused by the eruption of Thera comes from tree ring data from ancient bristlecone pines in California, some of the oldest living plants on the planet. These trees, and other buried tree limbs from Ireland, indicate a pronounced cooling period from 1630 to 1620 B.C.E. European and Turkish tree ring data have shown cooling between 1637 and 1628 B.C.E. Chinese records show that at this time there were unusual acidic fogs (probably sulfuric acid) and cold summers, followed by a period of drought and famine. The eruption of Thera therefore caused not only the destruction of the Minoan civilization, but also changed atmospheric conditions globally, forming frosts in California and killing tea crops in China.

The eruption of Thera seems to coincide with the fall of the Minoan civilization, certainly in the Santorini archipelago, but also on Crete and throughout the eastern Mediterranean. The cause of the collapse of the Minoan society was probably multifold, including earthquakes that preceded the eruption, ashfalls, and the 30-foot (9-m) tsunami waves that swept the eastern Mediterranean from the eruption. Since the Minoans were sea merchants, the tsunami would have devastated their fleet, harbor facilities, and coastal towns, causing such widespread destruction that the entire structure of their society fell apart. Vessels at sea would have been battered by the atmospheric pressure waves, covered in ash and pumice, and stranded in floating pumice far from ports. Crops were covered with ash, and palaces and homes were destroyed by earthquakes. The ash was acidic, so crops would have been ruined for years, leading to widespread famine and disease. People sought relief by leaving Crete, the homeland of the Minoan culture. Many of the survivors are thought to have migrated to Greece and North Africa, including the Nile Delta region, Tunisia, and the Levant, where the fleeing Minoans became known as the Philistines.

Vesuvius, 79 C.E.

The most famous volcanic eruption of all time is probably that of Vesuvius in the year 79 C.E. Mount Vesuvius is the only active volcano on the European mainland, towering 4,195 feet (1,279 m) above the densely populated areas of Naples, Ercolano, and surrounding communities in southern Italy. Vesuvius is an arc volcano related to the subduction of oceanic crust to the east of Italy beneath the Italian Peninsula. It rises from the plain of Campania between the Apennine Mountains to the east and the Tyrrhenian Sea to the west. The volcano developed inside the collapsed caldera of an older volcano known as Monte Somma, only a small part of which remains along the northern rim of Vesuvius. Monte Somma and Vesuvius have had at least five major eruptions in the past 4,000 years, including 1550 and 217 B.C.E., and 79, 472, and 1631 C.E. There have been at least 50 minor eruptions of Vesuvius since 79 C.E.

Ash from the 79 C.E. eruption buried the towns of Pompeii, Herculaneum, and Stabiae and killed tens of thousands of people. Before the eruption, Pompeii was a well-known center of commerce, home to approximately 20,000 people. The area was known for its wines, cabbage, and fish sauce and was a popular resort area for wealthy Roman citizens. Pompeii was a wealthy town, and the homes were elaborately decorated with statues, patterned tile floors, and frescoes on the walls. The city built a forum, several theaters, and a huge amphitheater in which 20,000 spectators could watch gladiators fight each other or animals, with the loser typically being killed.

A large caldera north of Vesuvius presently has molten magma moving beneath the surface resulting in a variety of volcanic phenomena that have inspired many legends. The Phlegraean Fields are the name given to a region where there are many steaming fumaroles spewing sulfurous gases and boiling mud pots, which may have inspired the Roman poet Virgil's description of the entrance to the underworld. The fumaroles are likened to the burning holes into which the ecclesiastical simonists were plunged headfirst and blasphemers, sodomites, and usurers were sentenced to walk on burning sands under a rain of fire. The land surface in the caldera rises and falls with the movement of magma below the surface. This is most evident near the sea where shorelines have moved up and down relative to coastal structures. At Pozzuoli, the ancient temple of Serapis lies partly submerged near the coast. The marble pillars on the temple show evidence of being previously submerged, as they are partly bored through by marine organisms, leaving visible holes in the pillars. Charles Lyell, in his famous treatise *Principles of Geology,* used this observation to demonstrate that land can subside and be uplifted relative to sea level. A few miles north of Pozzuoli, an ancient town known as Port Julius is completely beneath the sea, showing that *subsidence* has been ongoing for thousands of years.

Before the cataclysmic eruption in 79, the Campanians of southern Italy had forgotten that Vesuvius was a volcano and did not perceive any threat from the mountain, even though the geographer Strabo had 50 years earlier described many volcanic features from the mountain. The crater lake at the top of the mountain was used by the rebelling gladiator Spartacus and his cohorts to hide from the Roman army in 72 C.E., neither side aware of the danger of the crater. There were signs that the volcano was coming back to life. In the year 62, a powerful earthquake shook the region, damaging many structures and causing the water reservoir for Pompeii to collapse, flooding the town and killing and injuring many people. It is likely that poisonous volcanic gases also escaped through newly opened fractures at this time, as Roman historians and philosophers write of a flock of hundreds of sheep being mysteriously killed near Pompeii by a pestilence from within the Earth. (The descriptions are reminiscent of the carbon dioxide gases emitted from some volcanoes more recently, such as in the disasters of Lake Nyos in Cameroon in 1984 and 1986.) More earthquakes followed, including one in 63 that violently shook the theater where the emperor Nero was singing to a captive audience. Instead of evacuating the theater, Nero was convinced that his voice was ever stronger and perhaps excited the gods of the underworld.

On August 24, 79 C.E., Vesuvius erupted after several years of earthquakes. The initial blast launched 2.5 cubic miles (10 cubic km) of pumice, ash, and other volcanic material into the air, forming a mushroom cloud that expanded in the stratosphere. This first phase of the eruption lasted 12 hours, during which time Pompeii's terrified residents were pelted with blocks of pumice and a rain of volcanic ash that was falling on the city at a rate of 7–8 inches (15–20 cm) per hour. People were hiding in buildings and fleeing through the abnormally dark streets, many collapsing and dying from asphyxiation. Soon the weight of the ash was causing roofs to collapse on structures throughout the city, killing thousands more people. Pompeii was quickly buried under 10 feet (3 m) of volcanic debris. About half a day after the eruption began, the eruption column began to collapse from decreasing pressure from the magma chamber, and the eruption entered a new phase. At this stage, pyroclastic flows known as nuée ardents began flowing down the sides of the volcano. These flows consist of a mixture of hot gases, volcanic ash, pumice, and other particles and race downhill at hundreds of miles per hour while maintaining temperatures of 1,800°F (1,000°C) or more. These hot pyroclastic flows rip up and ignite anything in their path, and Herculaneum was first in their path.

Successive pyroclastic flows together killed about 4,000 people in Herculaneum and Vesuvius and neighboring towns following the initial blast. During the second phase of the massive eruption, huge quantities of ash were blown up to 20 miles (32 km) into the atmosphere, alternately surging upward and dropping tons of ash onto the surrounding region and killing most of the people who were not killed in the initial eruption. Daylight was quickly turned into a dark impenetrable night, and the town of Pompeii was buried under another 6–7 feet (~2 m) of ash. Thick ash also accumulated on the slopes of the volcano and was quickly saturated with water from rains created by the volcanic eruption. Water-saturated mudflows called lahars moved swiftly down the slopes of Vesuvius, burying the town of Herculaneum under additional volcanic layers up to 65 feet (20 m) thick and covering Pompeii by up to 20 feet (5 m) of mud. The towns of Herculaneum and Pompeii were not uncovered until archaeologists discovered their ruins nearly 2,000 years later when, in 1699, a scientist named Giuseppe Marcarini dug into an elevated mound and discovered parts of the buried city of Pompeii. However, in the early 1700s the public was not interested, and the region's history remained obscure. For the next century, wealthy landowners discovered that if they dug tunnels through the solidified ash they could find ancient statues, bronze pieces, and other valuable things that they used to decorate their homes. It was not until Italy became unified in 1860 and an archaeologist name Giuseppe Fiorelli was put in charge of excavations in southern Italy that looting changed to systematic excavation and study.

This area has been rebuilt, with farmland covering much of Pompeii and the town of Ercolano now lying on top of the 20 feet (6 m) of ash that buried Herculaneum. However, archaeological investigations at both sites have led to a wealth of information about life in ancient Italy. Pompeii in particular has proven to be a valuable time capsule preserved in pristine form by the encapsulating volcanic ash that entrapped so many people in homes and trying to escape in the streets. Vesuvius is still active and has experienced many eruptions since the famous erup-

(opposite page) (a) Map of Italy showing the location of Vesuvius and other active volcanoes of the Romana volcanic belt and the Aeolian volcanic complex, including Mount Etna. (b) Detailed image of Vesuvius showing lava flows (shaded) and locations of Pompeii and Herculaneum *(Modified after J. de Boer and D. Sanders)*

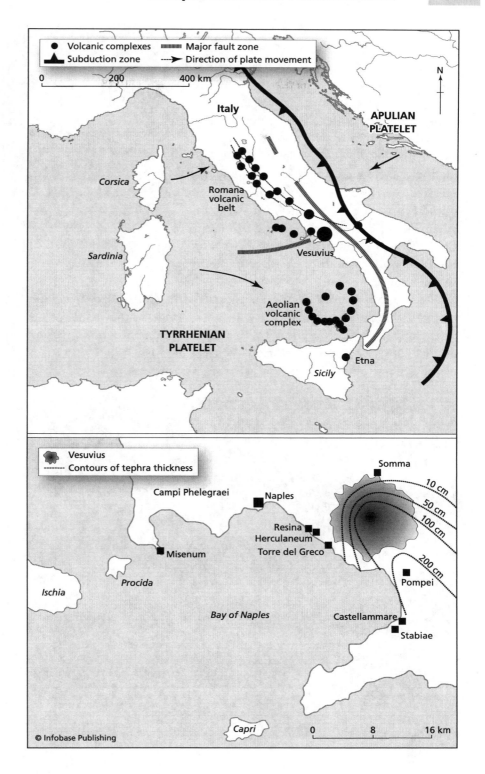

tion in 79 C.E. It is not recommended to visit Ercolano during an eruption of Vesuvius.

This famous eruption of Vesuvius in 79 C.E. is the source of some terms commonly used to describe features of volcanic eruptions. Pliny the Elder, the Roman naturalist and naval officer who was in charge of a squadron of vessels in the Bay of Naples during the eruption, commanded one of his vessels to move toward the mountain during the initial eruption for a better view and to rescue a friend. Both efforts failed, as the eruption was too intense to approach, so Pliny the Elder sailed south to Stabiae to attempt to save another friend. In Stabiae, Pliny the

Photo of Pompeii victim, propped up on forearms (Scala/Art Resource, New York)

Elder died, apparently from a heart attack brought on by struggling through the thick ash in the city. In an account of the death of his uncle and the eruption, Pliny the Elder's nephew, Pliny the Younger, described to the Roman historian Tacitus the mushroom cloud associated with the initial eruption as being like an umbrella where the

Historic sketch of Plinian column from Vesuvius, 79 C.E. (David A. Hardy/Photo Researchers, Inc.)

lower column rose up in a thin pipe and then expanded outward in all directions at the top. The term Plinian column is taken from these descriptions.

Tambora, Indonesia, 1815

The largest volcanic eruption ever recorded is that of the Indonesian *island arc* volcano Tambora in 1815. This eruption initially killed an estimated 92,000 people and sent so much particulate matter into the atmosphere that it influenced the climate of the planet, cooling the surface and changing patterns of rainfall globally. The year after the eruption is known as "the year without a summer" in reference to the global cooling caused by the eruption, although people at the time did not know the reason for the cooling. In cooler climates, the year without a summer saw snow throughout the summer and crops were not able to grow. Great masses of farmers in the United States moved from New England to the Midwest and Central Plains seeking a better climate for growing crops. This mass migration and population of the American Midwest was all because of a volcanic eruption on the other side of the world.

Tambora is located in Indonesia, a chain of thousands of islands that stretches from Southeast Asia to Australia. The tectonic origins of these islands are complex and varied, but many of the islands along the southwest part of the chain are volcanic in origin, formed above the Sumatra-Sunda trench system. Soils are fertile and host tropical rain forests, many of which have been deforested and replaced by tobacco, tea, coffee, and spice plantations (hence their nickname, the Spice Islands). This trench marks the edge of subduction of the Indian-Australia plates beneath the Philippine-Eurasian plates, and it formed a chain of convergent margin island arc volcanoes above the subduction zone. Tambora is one of these volcanoes, located on the island of Sumbawa, east of Java. Tambora is somewhat unique among the volcanoes of the Indonesian chain as it is located farther from the trench (210 miles/340 km) and farther above the subduction zone (110 miles/175 km) than other volcanoes in the chain. This is because Tambora is located at the junction of subducting continental crust from the Australian plate and subducting oceanic crust from the Indian plate. A major fault cutting across the convergent boundary is related to this transition, and the magmas that feed Tambora seem to have risen along fractures along this fault.

Tambora has a history of volcanic eruptions extending back at least 50,000 years. The age difference between successive volcanic layers is large, and there appears to have been as much as 5,000 years between individual large eruptions. This is a large time interval for most volcanoes and may be related to Tambora's unusual tectonic setting far from the trench along a fault zone related to differences between the types of material being subducted on either side of the fault.

In 1812, Tambora started reawakening with a series of earthquakes plus small steam and ash eruptions. People of the region did not pay much attention to these warnings, not remembering the ancient eruptions of 5,000 years ago. On April 5, 1815, Tambora erupted with an explosion that was heard 800 miles (1,300 km) away in Jakarta. Ash probably reached more than 15 miles (25 km) into the atmosphere, but this was only the beginning of what was to be one of history's greatest eruptions. Five days after the initial blast, a series of huge explosions rocked the island sending ash and pumice 25 miles (40 km) into the atmosphere and hot pyroclastic flows (nuée ardents) tumbling down the flanks of the volcano and into the sea. When the hot flows entered the cold water, steam eruptions sent additional material into the atmosphere, creating a scene of massive explosive volcanism and wreaking havoc on the surrounding land and marine ecosystems. More than 36 cubic miles (150 cubic km) were erupted during these explosions from Tambora, more than 100 times the volume of the Mount Saint Helens eruption of 1980.

Ash and other volcanic particles such as pumice from the April eruptions of Tambora covered huge areas that stretched many hundreds of miles across Indonesia. Towns located within a few tens of miles experienced hurricane force winds that carried rock fragments and ash, burying much in their path and causing widespread death and destruction. The ash was so dense it caused a darkness like night that lasted for days even in locations 40 miles (65 km) from the eruption center. Roofs collapsed from the weight of the ash, and 15-foot (4.5-m) tsunami waves were formed when the pyroclastic flows entered the sea. These tsunami swept far inland in low-lying areas, killing and sweeping away many people and livestock. A solid layer of ash, lumber, and bodies formed on the sea extending several miles west from the island of Sumbawa, and pieces of this floating mass drifted off across the Java Sea. Although it is difficult to estimate, at least 92,000 people were killed in this eruption. Crops were incinerated or poisoned, and irrigation systems destroyed, resulting in additional famine and disease after the eruption ceased, killing tens of thousands of people who survived the initial eruption and forcing hundreds of thousands of people to migrate to neighboring islands.

The atmospheric effects of the eruption of Tambora were profound. During the eruptions, Tambora shot huge amounts of sulfur dioxide and steam into the atmosphere and contaminated surface and groundwater systems. Much of the sulfur dioxide rained onto nearby lands and islands, causing diseases including persistent diarrhea. Huge amounts of gas also entered the upper atmosphere, causing changes to weather patterns throughout the world. In the upper atmosphere, sulfur dioxide combines with water molecules to form persistent sulfuric acid aerosols that reflect large amounts of sunlight back to space causing a global cooling effect. Weather data show that the Northern Hemisphere experienced temperatures as much as 10 degrees cooler than normal for three years following the eruption, and much of that cooling is attributed to the aerosols in the upper atmosphere. The Indian Ocean monsoon was disrupted to such an extent that some regions expecting rain were plagued with drought instead; then, when the rains were supposed to end, they finally came—but too late for the crops. Widespread famine followed by an epidemic of cholera engulfed northern India and surrounding areas (current-day Pakistan and Bangladesh). In eastern China, the Yangtze (Chang) and Yellow (Huang) Rivers suffered severe floods, destroying crops and killing many people. The cholera plague that started in India soon spread to Egypt, killing 12 percent of the population, then to Europe, where hundreds of thousands of people perished. The global outbreak soon spread to North America, hitting the immigrant cities of New York and Montreal particularly badly, where hundreds of people died each day. The cholera plague lasted from 1817 through 1823, representing one of the long-term secondary hazards of volcanic eruptions. The uncountable deaths resulting from the secondary effects of the eruption thus far outnumber the deaths from the initial eruption.

The year of 1816 is known as the year without a summer, caused by the atmospheric cooling from the sulfur dioxide released from Tambora. Snow fell in many areas across Europe, and in some places it was colored yellow and red from the volcanic particles in the atmosphere. Crops failed, people suffered, and social and economic unrest resulted from the poor weather. The Napoleonic wars soon erupted. Famine swept Europe hitting France especially hard, with food and antitax riots erupting in many places. The number of deaths from the famine in Europe is estimated at another 100,000 people.

North America also suffered from the global cooling brought on by Tambora. The New England states were hardest hit, experiencing a

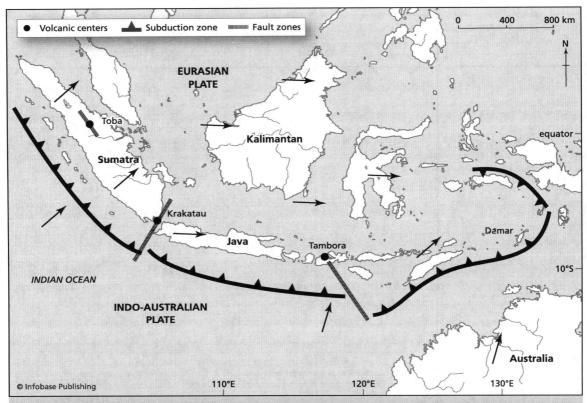

Map of Indonesia showing the locations of Tambora and Krakatau, both along faults above a subduction zone *(Modified after J. de Boer and D. Sanders)*

cold drought, with deep frosts and snowstorms hitting even in the typically hot months of June, July, and August. Crops failed, livestock had nothing to eat and perished, and many farmers resorted to fishing in streams to get food for their animals. Others were unable to cope with the loss of crops and rising food prices and became poor and dependent on charity. Others migrated to the fertile warmer plains of the American Midwest, expanding the country's wheat belt westward.

The eruption of Tambora illustrates the difficulty in estimating the numbers of deaths and the actual cost to the global population of a volcanic eruption. It is difficult enough to determine the deaths in remote areas that have been affected by a catastrophe of this magnitude, but when secondary effects such as disease, global epidemics, loss of crops, and changes of climate are taken into account, the numbers of those affected climbs by hundreds of thousands, millions, or more.

Krakatau, Indonesia, 1883

Indonesia has seen catastrophic volcanic eruptions other than Tambora. Indonesia has more volcanoes than any other country in the world, with more than 130 known active volcanoes. These volcanoes have been responsible for about one-third of all the deaths attributed to volcanic eruptions in the world. Indonesia stretches for more than 3,000 miles (5,000 km) between Southeast Asia and Australia and is characterized by very fertile soil, warm climate, and one of the densest populations on Earth. The main islands in Indonesia include, from northwest to southeast, Sumatra, Java, Kalimantan (formerly Borneo), Sulawesi (formerly Celebes), and the Sunda Islands. The country averages one volcanic eruption per month and, because of the dense population, it suffers approximately one-third of the world's fatalities from volcanic eruptions.

One of the most spectacular and devastating eruptions of all time was that of Krakatau, an uninhabited island in the Sunda Strait off the coast of the islands of Java and Sumatra, in 1883. This eruption generated a sonic blast that was heard thousands of miles away, spewed enormous quantities of ash into the atmosphere, and initiated a huge tsunami that killed roughly 40,000 people and wiped out more than 160 towns. The main eruption lasted for three days and the huge amounts of ash ejected into the atmosphere circled the globe and remained in the atmosphere for more than three years, forming spectacular sunsets and affecting global climate. Locally, the ash covered nearby islands killing crops, natural jungle vegetation, and wildlife, but most natural species returned within a few years.

Like Tambora, Krakatau is located at an anomalous location in the Indonesian arc. To the southeast of Krakatau, the volcanoes on the island of Java are aligned in an east-west direction, lying above the subducting Indo-Australian plate. To the northwest of Krakatau, volcanoes on Sumatra are aligned in a northwest-southeast direction. Krakatau is thus located at a major bend in the Indonesian arc and lies, along with a few other smaller volcanoes, above the Krakatau fault zone that strikes through the Sunda Strait. This fault zone is accommodating differential motion between Java and Sumatra. Java is moving east at 1.5 inches (4 cm per year), whereas Sumatra is moving northeast at 1.5 inches (4 cm per year) and rotating in a clockwise sense, resulting in a zone of oblique extension along the Krakatau fault zone in the Sunda Strait. The faults and fractures that have formed from this differential motion between the islands provide easy pathways for the magma and other fluids to migrate from great depths above the subduction zone to the surface. So, like Tambora, Krakatau has had unusually large volcanic eruptions and is located at an anomalous structural setting in the Indonesian arc.

Legends in the Indonesian islands discuss several huge eruptions from the Sunda Strait area, and geological investigations confirm many deposits and calderas from ancient events. Prior to the 1883 eruption, Krakatau consisted of several different islands including Perbuwatan in the north, Danan, and Rakata in the south. The 1883 eruption emptied a large underground magma chamber resulting in the formation of a large caldera complex. During the 1883 eruption, the islands of Perbuwatan, Danan, and half of Rakata collapsed into the caldera and sank below sea level. Since then a resurgent dome has grown out of the caldera, emerging above sea level as a new island in 1927. The new island is named Anak Krakatau (child of Krakatau), growing to repeat the cycle of cataclysmic eruptions in the Sunda Strait.

Prior to the 1883 eruption, the Sunda Strait was densely populated with many small villages built from bamboo and palm-thatched roofs. Krakatau is located in the middle of the strait, with the many starfish-shaped arms of the strait extending toward the islands of Sumatra and Java. Many villages, such as Telok Betong, lay at the ends of these progressively narrowing bays, pointed directly at Krakatau. These villages were popular stops for trading ships from the Indian Ocean to obtain supplies before heading through the Sunda Strait to the East Indies. The group of islands centered on Krakatau in the center of the strait was a familiar landmark for these sailors.

Although not widely appreciated as such at the time, the first signs that Krakatau was not a dormant volcano but was about to become very active appeared in 1860 and 1861 with small eruptions, then a series of earthquakes between 1877 and 1880. On May 20, 1883, Krakatau entered a violent eruption phase, witnessed by ships sailing through the Sunda Strait. The initial eruption sent a 7-mile- (11-km-) high plume above the strait, with the eruptions heard 100 miles (160 km) away in Jakarta. As the eruption expanded, ash covered villages in a 40-mile (60-km) radius. For several months, the volcano continued to erupt sporadically, covering the straits and surrounding villages with ash and pumice, while the earthquakes continued.

On August 26, the style of the eruptions took a severe turn for the worse. A series of extremely explosive eruptions sent an ash column 15 miles (25 km) into the atmosphere, sending many pyroclastic flows and nuée ardents spilling down the island's slopes and into the sea. A tsunami associated with the flows and earthquakes sent waves into the coastal areas surrounding the Sunda Strait, destroying or damaging many villages on Sumatra and Java. Ships passing through the straits were covered with ash, while others were washed ashore and shipwrecked by the many and increasingly large waves of the tsunami.

On August 27, Krakatau put on its final show, exploding with a massive eruption that pulverized the island and sent an eruption column 25 miles (40 km) into the atmosphere. The blasts from the eruption were heard as far away as Australia, the Philippines, and Sri Lanka. Atmospheric pressure waves broke windows on surrounding islands and traveled around the world as many as seven times, reaching the antipode, the area on the exact opposite side of the Earth from the eruption, at Bogatá, Colombia, 19 hours after the eruption. The amount of lava and debris erupted is estimated at 18–20 cubic miles (75–80 cubic km), making this one of the largest eruptions known in the past several centuries. Many sections of the volcano collapsed into the sea, forming steep-walled escarpments cutting through the volcanic core, some of which are preserved to this day. These massive landslides were related to the collapse of the caldera beneath Krakatau and contributed to the huge tsunami that ravaged the shores of the Sunda Strait, with waves

FIRSTHAND ACCOUNT OF THE ERUPTION OF KRAKATAU FROM A PASSENGER ON A PASSING SHIP

Some of the records of events during the cataclysmic eruptions came from passengers on ships in the Sunda Straits. One of these, from a passenger on the ship *Loudon* captained by Captain Lindemann, as it was anchored off the village of Telok Betong is as follows:

"Suddenly we saw a gigantic wave of prodigious height advancing toward the seashore with considerable speed. Immediately, the crew . . . managed to set sail in face of the imminent danger; the ship had just enough time to meet with the wave from the front. The ship met the wave head-on and the *Loudon* was lifted up with a dizzying rapidity and made a formidable leap . . . The ship rode at a high angle over the crest of the wave and down the other side. The wave continued on its journey toward land, and the benumbed crew watched as the sea in a single sweeping motion consumed the town. There, where an instant before had lain the town of Telok Betong, nothing remained but the open sea."

of average heights of 50 feet (15 m), although some reached up to 140 feet (40 m) where the V-shaped bays amplified wave height. Many of the small villages were swept away with no trace, boats were swept miles inland or ripped from their moorings, and thousands of residents in isolated villages in the Sunda Strait perished.

The tsunami was so powerful that many trees were ripped from the soil leaving only shattered stumps remaining as vestiges of the previous forest. In some places the forest was uprooted to elevations of 130 feet (40 m) above sea level. Bodies were strewn around the shores of the Sunda Strait and formed horrible scenes of death and destruction that survivors were not equipped to clean up. The population was decimated, food supplies and farmland were destroyed, and entire villages and roads were wiped off the islands or buried in deep layers of mud. Survivors were in a state of shock and despair after the disaster and soon had to deal with additional loss when disease and famine took

JAVANESE FARMWORKER'S FIRSTHAND ACCOUNT OF TSUNAMI

Firsthand accounts from people on nearby islands reveal the harrowing events that they had to experience. One such account, from a Javanese farmworker who was in the fields near the village of Merak (5 miles [8 km] inland on Java) during the eruption, is related below (after Scarth, 1999):

". . . all of a sudden there came a great noise. We . . . saw a great black thing, a long way off, coming towards us. It was very high and very strong, and we soon saw that it was water. Trees and houses were washed away . . . The people began to . . . run for their lives. Not far off was some steep sloping ground. We all ran towards it and tried to climb up out of the way of the water. The wave was too quick for most of them, and many were drowned almost at my side. . . . There was a general rush to climb up in one particular place. This caused a great block, and many of them got wedged together and could not move. Then they struggled and fought, screaming and crying out all the time. Those below tried to make those above them move on again by biting their heels. A great struggle took place for a few moments, but . . . one after another, they were washed down and carried far away by the rushing waters. You can see the marks on the hillside where the fight for life took place. Some . . . dragged others down with them. They would not let go their hold, nor could those above them release themselves from this death-grip."

over their lives. A state of anarchy ensued as rural people and farmers from the mountains descended to the coastal region and engaged in ganglike tribal looting and robbery, creating a state of chaos. Within a few months, however, troops sent by the colonial Dutch government regained control and began the rebuilding of the region. Nevertheless, many of the coastal croplands had their soil horizons removed and were not arable for many decades to come. Coastal reefs that served as fishing grounds were also destroyed, so without fishing or farming resources, many of the surviving residents moved inland.

Although it is uncertain how many people died in the volcanic eruption and associated tsunami, the Dutch colonial government estimated in 1883 that 36,417 people died, most of them (perhaps 90 percent) from the tsunami. Several thousand people were also killed by extremely powerful nuée ardents, or glowing clouds of hot ash, that raced across the Sunda Strait on cushions of hot air and steam. These clouds burned and suffocated all who were unfortunate enough to be in their direct paths.

Tsunamis from the eruption spread out across the Indian Ocean and caused destruction across much of the coastal regions of the entire Indian Ocean and around the world. Although documentation of this Indonesian tsunami is not nearly as good as that from the 2004 tsunami, many reports of the tsunami generated from Krakatau document this event. Residents of coastal India reported the sea suddenly receding to unprecedented levels, stranding fish that were quickly picked up by residents, many of whom were then washed away by large waves. The waves spread into the Atlantic Ocean and were detected in France, and a 7-foot (2-m) wave beached fishing vessels in Auckland, New Zealand.

Weeks after the eruption huge floating piles of debris and bodies were still found in the Sunda Strait, Java Strait, and Indian Ocean, providing grim reminders of the disaster to sailors in the area. Some areas were so densely packed with debris that sailors reported some regions appeared to look like solid ground, and people were able to walk across the surface. Fields of pumice from Krakatau reportedly washed up on the shores of Africa a year after the eruption, some even mixed with human skeletal remains. Other pumice rafts carried live plant seeds and species to distant shores, introducing exotic species across oceans that normally acted as barriers to plant migration.

Ash from the eruption fell for more than 1,500 miles (2,500 km) from the eruption for days after, and many fine particles remained in the atmosphere for years, spreading across the globe on atmospheric currents. The ash and sulfur dioxide from the eruption caused a low-

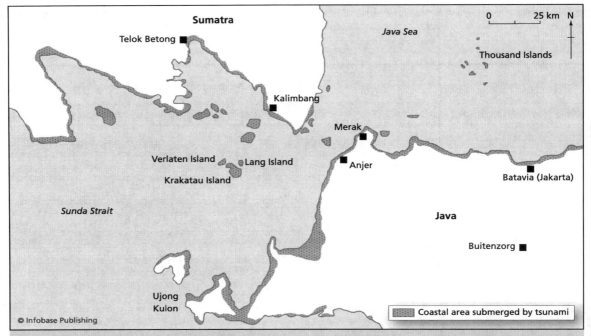

Map of the Sunda Strait in Indonesia, showing the location of Krakatau and the areas devastated by the huge tsunami generated by the 1883 eruption. Note how the bays with the worst damage are pointing toward the volcano and how they narrow progressively inland, amplifying the tsunami. *(Modified from P. Francis)*

ering of global temperatures by several degrees and created many spectacular sunsets and atmospheric light phenomena by reflected and refracted sunlight through the particles and gas emitted into the atmosphere.

On western Java, one of the most densely populated regions in the world, destruction on the Ujong Kulon Peninsula was so intense that the peninsula was designated a national park as a reminder of the power and continued potential for destruction from Krakatau. Such designations of hazardous coastal and other areas of potential destruction as national parks and monuments is good practice for decreasing the severity of future natural eruptions and processes.

In the years after the eruption stripped Krakatau and nearby islands of vegetation, biologists were able to study the sequence and mechanisms by which fauna and flora repopulate devastated lands. Birds, spiders, seeds in bird guano, and windblown seeds first attempted to establish a foothold on the barren islands, then water-drifted plants and even animals followed. A little more than a year after the eruption, grasses were beginning to take root, and, by three years after the eruption, dozens of species of plants were found on the islands. Forty years after the eruption, small stands of forest were established, and zones of grasses and ferns could be found going upslope from the shore. With time, the number of different species increased, and eventually animals appeared, having a plant community that was able to sustain their diet. By 1929, several species of mammals, birds, and reptiles were found on the islands, including crocodiles, snakes, and lizards.

Agricultural productivity remained low for many decades following the 1883 eruption. Forty years after the eruption, crop productivity was only about 30 percent of pre-eruption levels, and, by 1927, the crops' yields were only up to 50 percent.

Krakatau began rebuilding new cinder cones that emerged from beneath the waves in 1927 through 1929, when the new island, named Anak Krakatau (child of Krakatau), went into a rapid growth phase. Several cinder cones have now risen to heights approaching 600 feet (190 m) above sea level. The cinder cones will undoubtedly continue to grow until Krakatau's next catastrophic caldera collapse eruption.

Conclusion

Historical accounts of ancient eruptions reveal a huge range in the character of each volcano and of the types of processes that have led to the largest loss of life. Despite this, it is clear from the many examples discussed here that large volcanic eruptions typically are preceded by periods of earthquakes, small eruptions, emissions of gas, and other phenomena that should be heeded as a warning for residents to leave the areas closest to a volcano to save their lives. Most lives have been lost through burial of villages, towns, and cities in hot, fast-moving ash clouds called nuée ardents, burial under thick ash blankets, or by being crushed and swept away by volcanic-induced tsunami. The largest volcanic eruptions, such as those of Santorini, Tambora, and Krakatau, can cause global climate changes that induce drought and disease, global cooling, or, in some cases, warming that have affected the entire planet. The eruption of Krakatau is thought to be indirectly responsible for global outbreaks of cholera and other diseases that killed millions of people, and, in this way, secondary effects of eruptions can be more catastrophic than the local devastating effects.

5

Examples of Volcanic Disasters of the Twentieth and Twenty-first Centuries

Just as it was informative to examine some of history's greatest eruptions, it is instructive to study some of the most significant eruptions of the 20th and 21st centuries. By doing so, it is possible to see how better observational and monitoring tools, as well as knowledge of past eruptions, may have saved lives. This is most evident from the eruption of Mount Pinatubo in the Philippines, one of the largest eruptions of the century, but one that was heavily monitored, saving thousands of lives.

Mount Pelée, Martinique, 1902

Martinique is a quiet island in the West Indies first discovered by Columbus in 1502. Its native Carib people were killed off or assimilated into the black slave population brought over by French colonizers to run the sugar, tobacco, and coffee plantations. The city of Saint-Pierre on the northwest side of the island became the main seaport, as well as the cultural, educational, and commercial center. The city became known as the "Paris of the West Indies," with many rum distilleries, red-roofed white masonry buildings, banks, schools, and beautiful beaches, all framed by a picturesque volcano in the background.

The island is part of the Lesser Antilles arc, sitting above a west-dipping subduction zone built on the eastern margin of the Caribbean plate. The oceanic crust of the Atlantic Ocean basin that is part of the North American plate is being pushed beneath the Caribbean plate at about 1 inch (2 cm) per year. The oldest volcanoes on Martinique, including Morne Jacob, the Pitons du Carbet, and Mount Conil, emerged from the sea about 3–4 million years ago. They were built on a submarine island arc that had been active for approximately the last 16 million years. Pelée is a much younger volcano, first known to have erupted about 200,000 years ago. It rises to a height of 4,580 feet (1,397 m) on the north end of the island and has had major historic eruptions in 65 B.C.E., 280, and 1300, and smaller eruptions about every 50 to 150 years. Mount Pelée is located uphill and only 6 miles (10 km) from the port city of Saint-Pierre, located along the northwestern coast of the island. It derives its name from the French word for "bald" (or "peeled"), after the eruptions of 1792 and 1851 that removed all vegetation from the top of the volcano.

Mount Pelée began to awake slowly in 1898 when sulfurous gases were noticed coming out of a crater on the top of the mountain and in the Rivière Blanche that flows through a gorge on the southwest flank of the volcano. Minor eruptions of steam became abundant in 1901, and additional gaseous emissions were common as well. In the spring of 1902, Mount Pelée began to show increased activity, with boiling lakes and intermittent minor pyroclastic flows and eruptions, associated with minor earthquake activity. All these phenomena were associated with the rise of magma beneath the volcano and were warnings about the upcoming eruption. A dome of magma began growing in one of the craters on top of the volcano and then a huge, 650-foot- (200-m-) wide tower of solidified magma known as the spine formed a plug that rose to 375 feet (115 m) before the catastrophic May 8 eruption.

By April, most people were becoming worried about the increasingly intense activity and were congregating in the city of Saint-Pierre to catch boats to leave the island. Saint-Pierre was located only 6 miles (9 km) from the volcano. Landslides in the upper Rivière Blanche triggered a series of massive mudflows that rushed down the river, while others crashed down the valley when water in the crater lake in l'Etang Sec, the main volcanic vent on Pelée, broke through a crack in the crater rim and escaped down the flank of the volcano. These landslides and mudflows were probably triggered by minor seismic activity associated with magma rising upward beneath Pelée. On May 3, groundwater began rushing out of fissures that opened in the ground and carried soil, trees, and carcasses of dead animals down through Saint-Pierre and out to sea. Flooding was widespread and destroyed many farms and villages, such as Le Prêcheur, carrying the wreckage downstream.

On May 4, a fissure opened in the ground in the village of Ajoupa-Bouillon northeast of Pelée and caused a huge steam and mud eruption that killed several people. Floods and mudflows continued to flow down other rivers, including those that passed through Saint-Pierre. Submarine landslides ruptured communication cables and carried them to depths of 0.5 mile (0.7 km). A larger eruption occurred on May 5 and killed 40 people in a pyroclastic flow that raced down the Rivière Blanche. Residents desperately wanted to leave the island to get to safety. However, elections were five days away, and Governor Louis Mouttet did not want the island's people to leave, for fear he might lose the election in a bad turnout. He ordered the military to halt the exodus from the island. Governor Mouttet was running as the head of the békés, an ultra-conservative white supremacist party being opposed by a new mixed-race socialist party that was becoming increasingly powerful. A successful election for the socialists would have changed the balance of power in Martinique and other French colonies and was resisted by many means (likely including election fraud) by the ruling békés. By this stage, precursors to the eruption included strange

FIRSTHAND ACCOUNT OF LAHARS OF MOUNT PELÉE, 1902

The terror of the mudflows flowing down Mount Pelée's flanks has been captured by a firsthand account written by a Dr. Auguste Guérin (related in Alwyn Scarth, 1999), who owned a factory near the Rivière Blanche.

"Then I heard a noise that I can't compare with anything else—an immense noise—like the devil on Earth! A black avalanche, beneath white smoke, an enormous mass, full of huge blocks, more than 10m high and at least 150 m wide, was coming down the mountain with a great din. It . . . rolled up against the factory like an army of giant rams. I was rooted to the spot.

My unfortunate son and his wife ran away from it toward the shore . . . All at once, the mud arrived. It passed 10 m in front of me. I felt its deathly breath. There was a great crashing sound. Everything was crushed, drowned and submerged. My son, his wife, thirty people and huge buildings were all swept away . . . Three of those black waves came down . . . making a noise like thunder, and made the sea retreat. Under the impact of the third wave, a boat moored in the factory harbour was thrown . . . over a factory wall, killing one of my foremen, who was standing next to me. I went down to the shore. The desolation was indescribable. Where a prosperous factory—the work of a lifetime—had stood a moment before, there was now nothing left but an expanse of mud forming a black shroud for my son, his wife, and my workmen."

behavior by animals and insects. A plague of armies of ants, venomous centipedes, poisonous snakes including pit vipers, and mammals began migrating in mass down the flanks of the volcano and invaded villages, plantations, and Saint-Pierre to the horror of residents. These insects and animals attacked people in factories, plantations, and homes, injuring and killing many. Poisonous gases killed birds in flight, which dropped on towns like ominous warnings from the sky. Mudflows continued down the volcano flanks and now included boiling lahars, one of which tore down the Rivière Blanche killing many people in factories and homes in the boiling mixture of mud, ash, and water. Other people in Saint-Pierre were dying rapidly of a contagious boil-like plague caused by drinking water contaminated by ash and sewage.

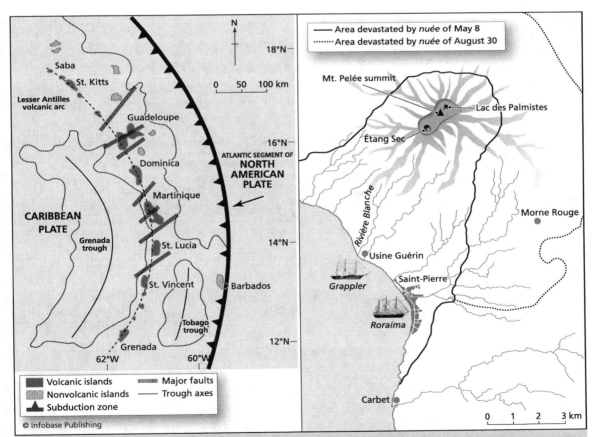

(a) Map of the Caribbean and the Lesser Antilles arc, showing the location of Martinique along a fault above a subduction zone. *(Map modified from J. de Boer and D. Sanders, 2002)* (b) Map of the area around Saint-Pierre and Mount Pelée on Martinique devastated by the 1902 eruption. *(Modified from P. Francis)*

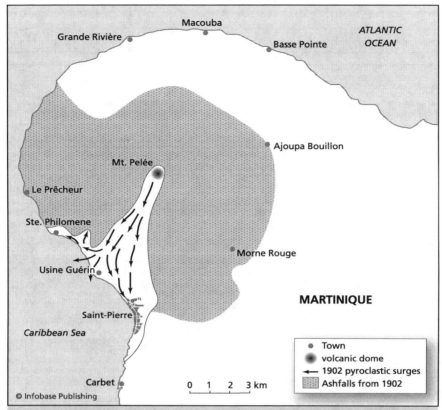

Map of the pyroclastic flows from the 1902 eruptions, in relation to the dome of Mount Pelée and cities and settlements including Saint-Pierre, Carbet, and Le Prêcheur

Workers on the docks went on strike, and there was little chance for anybody to escape the condemned city.

On May 6, residents of the city, now in a state of turmoil, woke to a new layer of ash covering city streets and fields. However, this ash was not from Pelée, but from another massive eruption that occurred overnight 80 miles (130 km) to the south on the British colony island of St. Vincent where the volcano La Soufrière killed 1,650 residents of that island. The Soufrière eruption triggered submarine slides that broke all communication lines to and from Martinique, totally isolating that island from the world during the disaster that was about to occur. Ironically, communication lines to St. Vincent remained intact, and surviving residents on St. Vincent were able to dispatch cables to England for help. Ships were dispatched from England, but when they arrived they assumed all the ash and debris in the water was from St. Vincent and help was not sent to Saint-Pierre until much later when it was realized that two major eruptions had occurred from two different volcanoes.

On May 7, the volcano was thundering with loud explosions that were heard throughout the Lesser Antilles. Smoke, fires, and flashes of lightning made for a frightening spectacle, especially at night when the fires reflected off the low-lying clouds and ash. Volcanic bombs were being spewed from Pelée and landing on homes and fields on the outskirts of Saint-Pierre, starting many fires. Governor Mouttet and his wife visited Saint-Pierre from the capital of Fort-de-France to try to convince residents that it was safe to remain and to vote in the elections. However, at 7:50 A.M. on May 8, several huge sonic blasts rocked the island and a tall eruption column rose quickly from the top of the volcano. A few minutes later, a huge nuée ardent erupted from Mount Pelée at 2,200°F (900°C) and moved over the six miles to Saint-Pierre at 115 miles (185 km) per hour (some estimates are as high as 310 miles (500 km) per hour), reaching the city 10 minutes after the eruption began. This began as a lateral blast or a collapse of the eruption column, aimed directly at Saint-Pierre below. As the pyroclastic flow rushed down the mountain, it expanded and scorched forests, sugarcane fields, and villages on the flanks of the volcano. The temperature of the flow cooled to an estimated 410–780°F (200–400°C) by the time it reached the sea, but this was enough to burn almost anything in its path. When the hot ash cloud reached Saint-Pierre, it demolished buildings and ignited flash fires throughout the city. Thousands of casks of rum stored in the city ignited and flowed as rivers of fire to the sea, burning at temperatures high enough to melt glass. The eruption cloud continued past the city and screamed over the harbor on a cushion of hot steam, overturning and burning many ships at anchor, sending them to the seafloor and killing most sailors on board.

Many accounts of the eruption say that all but two of the city's 30,000 residents were killed. Although about 30 residents survived the initial eruption, more than 27,000 were killed in the first massive eruption. Most died in a matter of minutes during passage of the ash cloud, but others died slowly of suffocation from ash or volcanic gas. One of the survivors was a prisoner named Auguste Ciparis who had been jailed for fighting and was spending his jail term in a deep dungeonlike cell that sheltered him from the hot ash cloud. Auguste spent the rest of his life being paraded to freak shows around the United States by the Barnum & Bailey circus to show his badly burned body as "The Prisoner of Saint-Pierre." About 2,000 people from surrounding towns were killed

FIRSTHAND ACCOUNTS OF NUÉE ARDENT HITTING SAINT-PIERRE, 1902

There are many eyewitness accounts of the eruption and nuée ardent, mainly from some of the sailors who were anchored at sea during the eruption and witnessed the fury of Pelée. One such account is from assistant purser Thompson, who was aboard the steamship *Roraima* that had just arrived at Saint-Pierre that morning. He wrote:

I saw Saint-Pierre destroyed. It was blotted out by one great blast of fire. Nearly 40,000 persons were all killed at once. Out of 18 vessels lying in the roads (the harbor) only one, the British steamer *Roddam*, escaped, and she, I hear, lost more than half on board. It was a dying crew that took her out.

"Our boat . . . arrived at Saint Pierre early Thursday morning. For hours before we entered the roadstead we could see flames and smoke rising from Mont Pelée. No one on board had any idea of danger. Captain G. T. Muggah was on the bridge, and all hands got on deck to see the show.

The spectacle was magnificent. As we approached Saint-Pierre we could distinguish the rolling and leaping of the red flames that belched from the mountain in huge volumes and gushed high into the sky. Enormous clouds of black smoke hung over the volcano.

When I anchored at Saint-Pierre I noticed the cable steamer *Grappler*, the *Roddam*, three or four American schooners, and a number of Italian and Norwegian barks. The flames were then spurting straight up into the air, now and then waving to one side or the other for a moment and again leaping suddenly higher up.

There was a constant muffled roar. It was like the biggest oil refinery in the world burning up on the mountain-top. There was a tremendous explosion about 7:45 o'clock, soon after we got in. The mountain was blown to pieces. There was no warning. The side of the mountain was ripped out, and there was hurled toward us a solid wall of flames. It sounded like thousands of cannon.

The wave of fire was on us like a lightning flash. It was like a hurricane of fire. I saw it strike the . . . *Grappler* broadside on and capsize her. From end to end she burst into flames and then sank. The fire rolled in mass straight down upon Saint-Pierre and the shipping docks. The town vanished before our eyes and the air grew stifling hot, and we were in the thick of it.

Wherever the mass of fire struck the sea the water boiled and sent up vast clouds of steam. The sea was torn into huge whirlpools that careened toward the open sea. One of the horrible hot whirlpools swung under the *Roraima* and pulled her down on her beam ends with the suction. She careened way over to port, and then the fire hurricane from the volcano smashed her, and over she went on the opposite side. The fire wave swept off the mast and smokestack as if they were cut with a knife.

(continues)

in later eruptions. Governor Mouttet and his wife were buried in the flow and were never seen again.

After the catastrophic eruption, magma continued to rise through the volcano and formed a new dome that rose above the crater's rim by the end of the month, and the spine rose to a height of 1,000 feet (300 m). Another pyroclastic eruption followed the same path on May 20, burning anything that had escaped the first eruption. Small erup-

(continued)

Captain Muggah was the only one on deck not killed outright. He was caught by the fire wave and terribly burned. He yelled to get up the anchor, but, before two fathoms were heaved, the *Roraima* was almost upset by the boiling whirlpool and the fire wave had thrown her down on her beam ends to seaboard. Captain Muggah was overcome by the flames. He fell unconscious from the bridge and toppled overboard.

The blast of fire from the volcano lasted only a few minutes. It shriveled and set fire to everything it touched. Thousands of casks of rum were stored in Saint-Pierre, and these were exploded by the terrific heat. The burning rum ran in streams down every street and out to sea. This blazing rum set fire to the *Roraima* several times. Before the volcano burst the landings of Saint-Pierre were crowded with people. After the explosion not one living being was seen on land. Only 25 of those on the *Roraima* out of 68 were left after the first flash.

The French cruiser *Suchet* came in and took us off at 2 P.M. She remained nearby, helping all she could, until 5 o'clock, then went to Fort de France with all the people she had rescued. At the time it looked as if the entire north end of the island was on fire."

The scene of destruction was summarized in a passage written by Monsieur Paral, the vicar-general of Martinique, when he visited Saint-Pierre about one day after the eruption (quoted in Peter Francis, 1993).

"Thursday 8 May. Ascension Day. This date should be written in blood . . . When, at about 3:00 in the afternoon we rounded the last promontory which separated us from what was once the magnificent panorama of Saint-Pierre, we suddenly perceived at the opposite extremity of the roadstead the Rivière Blanche with its crest of vapour, rushing madly into the sea. Then a little further out blazes a great American packet (the *Roraima*), which arrived on the scene just in time to be overwhelmed by the catastrophe. Nearer the shore, two other ships are in flames. The coast is strewn with wreckage, with the keels of overturned boats, all that remains of the twenty to thirty ships which lay at anchor here the day before. All along the quays, for a distance of 200 meters, piles of lumber are burning. Here and there around the city . . . fires can be seen through the smoke. But Saint-Pierre, in the morning throbbing with life, thronged with people, is no more. Its ruins stretch before us, wrapped in their shroud of smoke and ashes, gloomy and silent, a city of the dead. Our eyes seek out the inhabitants fleeing distracted, or returning to look for the dead. Nothing to be seen. No living soul appears in this desert of desolation, encompassed by appalling silence."

tions continued to cover the region with ash, until activity subsided in July 1905.

The 1902 eruption of Pelée was the first clearly documented example of a nuée ardent, or hot glowing avalanche cloud. Successive eruptions of Mount Pelée in 1904 provided additional documentation of this eruption style and the dangers it posed to all in its path. Even though the amount of magma released in these flows may be relatively small, the destructiveness of these hot, fast-moving flows is dramatic.

The 1902 eruption of Pelée highlights once again the bad side of human nature following major disasters. After the eruption, many robbers and looters descended on the region looking for jewels and other valuables and terrorizing people in the countryside who had managed to escape the volcano's fury. French troops battled the bands of thieves for months before order was restored and relative peace returned to the grave-city of Saint-Pierre. The island was made a *departement* of France in 1946. Today, the whole region is resettled and densely inhabited. The West Indies arc is still active and similar hazards remain to this day.

Nuée ardent photographed flowing down Mount Pelée on December 16, 1902 *(Library of Congress)*

Lake Nyos, Cameroon, 1986

Cameroon is an equatorial country sitting on Africa's Gulf of Guinea south of the Niger delta. A series of volcanoes forms a chain of peaks known as the Cameroon volcanic line trending northeast from the coast and extending as a line of volcanic peaks into the Atlantic Ocean. Many of these volcanoes have deep crater lakes on their summits and flanks, filled by rains that drench the jungle landscape. One crater, Lake Nyos, was formed from a relatively recent explosive gas eruption that blasted through bedrock and is now more than a mile (1.6 km) across and nearly 700 feet (220 m) deep. Thus, Nyos is not a volcano built by constructive volcanic processes, but a crater blasted by a gas-rich eruption. It is a strikingly beautiful crater, with deep blue water surrounded by lush green tropical vegetation on rugged hills.

At 9:30 P.M. on August 21, 1986, Lake Nyos trembled and a low rumble of uncertain origin was heard from the mountain and was soon followed by the emission of a huge and deadly cloud of toxic gas that flowed down the flanks of the volcano, suffocating 1,700 people and approximately 3,000 head of cattle, plus untold numbers of other animals. The gas formed dense cloudy fingers of gas up to 200 feet (50 m) thick that swept through valleys at speeds of up to 45 MPH (72 km/hr), initially overcoming people with fatigue, dizziness, and confusion, before they lapsed into comas and death. Few escaped the poisonous fumes, yet

View of Saint-Pierre devastated by the 1902 eruption, with Mount Pelée in the background *(Library of Congress)*

unlike volcanic eruptions, this gas emission did not disturb the vegetation or landscape.

The gas cloud was formed of carbon dioxide, a gas that is not toxic in normal concentrations, but was so concentrated that it was deadly. Since carbon dioxide is heavier than air, it hugged the ground and displaced the oxygen-rich layer that animals and people need to survive.

The gas that erupted from Nyos on the night of August 21 originated as a dense layer at the bottom of the lake, accumulated from gradual leaking from basaltic magma at depth. Deep lakes are often stratified (layered), where a dense lower layer or layers can hold high quantities of dissolved gas, held under pressure by the weight of the overlying water. The phenomenon is analogous to the carbon dioxide dissolved in soda or other carbonated beverages that bubbles out when the top is opened and the pressure released. When the concentration of gas gets to be very high, the mass of gas-rich water becomes unstable and small disturbances can set off a catastrophic release of gas. When a bubble is released it moves with increasing speed as it moves upward, setting off more and more bubbles as it rises through the unstable column. It is estimated that some disturbance (e.g., a gas release from magma below, an earthquake, or *slump*) set off an initial gas release that set off a chain reaction. By the time the coalesced bubbles reached the surface, they formed a stream of gas a cubic mile in volume moving upward at 200 MPH (320 km/hr). When the gas reached the surface the gas was heavier than the air and flowed down the flanks of the mountain killing all that require oxygen to survive.

The eruption released about 66 percent of the gas dissolved at depth and lowered the lake level by more than 3 feet (1 m). The lake was muddy and disturbed from the overturning of the deep waters and only gradually returned to its pre-eruption state. The exact trigger of the overturn and release of the gas is not known, but may be related to a seasonal instability in deep stratified lakes. Lakes in this region are the most unstable in August, and indeed a similar gas eruption from the nearby crater of Lake Monoun on August 15, 1984, killed 37 people.

Emissions of gas will continue in this region, and local governments are taking some action to try to prevent similar loss of life. Alarm systems could be installed, but, more important, preventative measures are being implemented. For instance, deep pipes are being installed into the lake, to slowly take the deep gases out of the lower lake levels, releasing the carbon dioxide slowly and harmlessly into the atmosphere before it builds up to deadly and catastrophic levels.

Nevado del Ruiz, Colombia, 1985

The most deadly volcanic-induced disaster of modern times started with a relatively minor eruption in the Andes of South America. The Nevado del Ruiz volcano in Colombia entered an active phase in November 1984 and began to show harmonic tremors on November 10, 1985. At 9:37 P.M. that night, a large Plinian eruption sent an ash cloud several miles into the atmosphere, and this ash settled onto the ice cap on top of the mountain. The ash, together with volcanic steam, quickly melted large amounts of ice, which then mixed with the ash and formed giant lahars (mudflows) that swept down the east side of the mountain into the village of Chinchina, killing 1,800 people. The eruption continued and melted more ice that mixed with more ash and sent additional and larger lahars westward. Some of these lahars moved at nearly 30 MPH (50 km/hr) and, with a thunderous roar, buried the town of Armero under 26 feet (8 m) of mud. Twenty-two thousand people died in Armero that night. Many could have been saved, since warnings were issued before the mudflow, but went unheeded.

Nevado del Ruiz had gone through a year of intermittent precursory activity that indicated that an eruption might occur, and the volcano was being studied by a group of Colombian geologists at the time of the eruption. At 3:05 P.M. on November 13, 1985, ranchers north of the volcano heard a low, rumbling noise and about two hours later observed a plume of black ash rise from the volcano and fall on the town of Armero 45 miles (72 km) away. By 4 P.M., local civil defense officials warned that an eruption was in progress and recommended that towns including Armero, Honda, and others be ready for immediate evacuation. After several hours of meetings, the Red Cross ordered the evacuation of Armero at 7:30 P.M. Residents may not have heard the warnings or understood the danger moving their way.

At 9:08 P.M., two large explosions marked the start of a larger eruption, associated with a series of pyroclastic flows and surges that moved

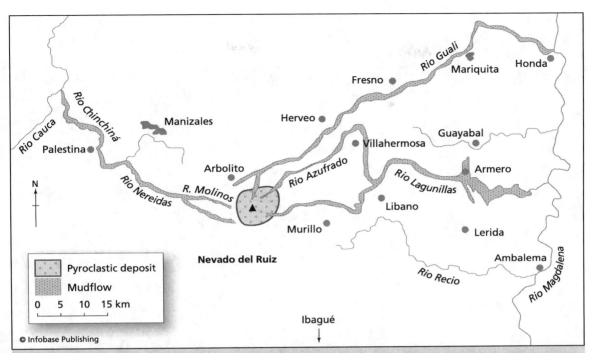

Map of Nevado del Ruiz and towns devastated by volcanic-induced mudflows in 1985, including Armero *(Modified from P. Francis)*

down the north flank of the volcano. The volcanic deposits moved across the ice cap on the mountain, scouring, melting, and covering it in various places. This released large amounts of meltwater mixed with debris that moved down the slopes, quickly forming giant lahars that scoured the channels of the Nereidas, Molinos, Gualí, Azufrado, and Lagunillas rivers and picking up huge amounts of debris including rocks, soil, and vegetation in the process.

At 9:30 P.M., a Plinian eruption column was visible, rising to nearly 7 miles (11 km) and hurling blocks and bombs of andesitic pumice up to a couple of miles from the crater, with ash falling up to 250 miles (400 km) away. At 10:30 P.M., lahars began sweeping through the village of Chinchina, and additional warnings were sent to Armero. Later, survivors reported that electricity was out sporadically and many residents may not have heard the warnings. At 11:30 P.M., giant lahars surged into Armero in successive waves moving at 22–30 MPH (35–50 km/hr), sweeping away homes, cars, people, and livestock and embedding all in 26 feet (8 m) of mud. Many people survived the initial inundation but were trapped half-buried in the mud and died later of exposure.

Photos of mudflow from Nevado del Ruiz volcano that buried the town of Armero. The mud flowed out of the mountains in the background and covered the town in the foreground. *(Jacques Langevin/Corbis Sygma)*

Scientists have learned many lessons from Nevado del Ruiz that could be useful to save lives in the future. First, even minor volcanic eruptions can trigger catastrophic mudflows under the right conditions, and geologic hazard maps should be made in areas of volcanism to understand the hazards and help emergency planning in times of eruption. Local topographic variations can focus lahars, enhancing their lethality in some places and spreading them out in others. Armero was located at the end of canyon that focused the worst parts of the flow in the heart of the village. Understanding past hazards can help understand what may happen in the future. If geologists had helped plan the location of Armero, they would have noticed that the town was on top of an older lahar deposit that swept down the mountain in 1845, also killing all inhabitants more than a century earlier. Apparently the geologic record shows a number of repeated mudflows destroying villages at the site of Armero. A final lesson from Armero is that warning systems need to be in place, and even simple alarm systems can save thousands of lives.

If residents of Armero had had even an hour warning they could have fled to the valley slopes and survived. The mudflows traveled 45 miles (70 km), taking about one-and-a-half hours to get to Armero, so even simple warnings could have saved lives.

Mount Saint Helens, 1980, and the Cascades Today

The most significant eruption in the conterminous United States in the past 90 years was that of Mount Saint Helens in 1980, a mountain that had lain dormant for 123 years. The volcano is part of the active Cascade volcanic arc, a continental margin arc built on the western coast of North America above where the small Juan de Fuca plate is being subducted beneath North America. The arc is relatively small (about 1,200 miles [2,000 km]) and stretches from Lassen Peak in California to Mount Garibaldi in British Columbia. Cascade volcanoes in the United States include Lassen Peak, Mount Shasta, Crater Lake, the Three Sisters, Mount Jefferson, Mount Hood, Mount Adams, Mount Saint Helens, and Mount Rainier. Commander George Vancouver of the British navy, while exploring the Spanish-claimed Pacific northwest, named Mount Saint Helens and other peaks of the Cascades in 1792. Mount Saint Helens was known as Loo-Wit by the native tribes and was named Saint Helens after Baron Saint Helens (aka Alleyene Fitzherbert), the British ambassador to Spain. Significant volcanic threats remain from Mount Saint Helens, Mount Rainier, and other Cascade volcanoes, especially in the densely populated Seattle area.

Mount Saint Helens began to grow above the Cascadia subduction zone about 50,000 years ago, and the volcanic cone that blew up in 1980 formed about 2,500 years ago. In the time since its birth, Mount Saint Helens has been one of the most active Cascade volcanoes, erupting on average every 40 to 140 years. However, the largest eruption from a Cascade volcano was from the present site of Crater Lake. A volcano known as Mount Mazama occupied this site about 6,000 years ago, but exploded in a cataclysmic eruption that covered much of the Pacific Northwest with volcanic ash. As the crust above the emptied magma chamber collapsed, a giant caldera formed, now occupied by the 2,000-foot- (610-m-) deep Crater Lake in Oregon. If such a huge volcanic eruption were to occur today in the densely populated Pacific Northwest the effects would be devastating, and many thousands of people would die. The landscape would be covered with choking ash, rivers would be filled with mudflows, and the global climate would be adversely affected for years.

Aerial view of eruption of Mount Saint Helens, Skamania County, Washington, May 18, 1980 *(USGS)*

As the Pacific Northwest became densely settled, the natural areas around Mount Saint Helens became popular recreation and tourist sites, attracting many to the beautiful scenery. On March 20, 1980, the mountain rumbled with a magnitude 4.1 earthquake, prompting geologists from the USGS to install a variety of volcano-monitoring equipment. Automatic cameras, seismographs, tilt meters, gravity meters, and gas collectors were installed to monitor the volcano for any new signs of impending eruption. A variety of precursory warnings of an impending eruption were observed, the most important of which were many swarms of closely spaced small earthquakes known as harmonic tremors and a seismic humming of the volcano. The USGS and Forest Service began to consider volcanic hazards in the area and to propose evacuation routes in case of disaster.

On March 27, 1980, many small eruptions on Mount Saint Helens were initiated when magma rose high enough to meet groundwa-

Aerial view of timber blown down by the horizontal blast of Mount Saint Helens on May 18, 1980 *(R. E. Wallace, USGS)*

ter, which caused steam explosions to reach about 2 miles (3 km) into the sky. The volcano gradually bulged by about 300 feet (90 m), and harmonic tremors indicated an impending large eruption. By this time, several small craters on the volcano's summit had merged to form a single, large crater 1,600 feet (500 m) across and 900 feet (1,600 feet) deep. The USGS issued eruption warnings, the governor declared a state of emergency, and the area was evacuated.

The bulge on the volcano continued to grow and the USGS established a volcano-monitoring station 6 miles (10 km) from the summit, while the government declared an area around the summit off-limits to all unauthorized personnel.

At 8:32 A.M. on May 18, 1980, the upper 1,313 feet (394 m) of the volcano were blown away in an unusual lateral blast. A magnitude 5.1 earthquake initiated the lateral blast, causing parts of the bulge to collapse and slide away in three separate landslides. The rocks mixed with snow and debris forming a huge debris avalanche that raced down the mountain at 150 MPH (200 km/hr), in one of the largest debris avalanches ever recorded. More than 1 cubic mile (4 cubic km) of material moved downhill in the debris avalanche, most of which remain in and around Spirit Lake in layers up to 300 feet (90 m) thick, forming a dam at the outlet of the lake that raised the lake level 200 feet (60 m), doubling its size. The blast from the eruption created a sonic boom that was heard up to 500 miles (800 km) away in Montana, yet people very close to the volcano heard nothing. This is because the sound waves from the eruption initially moved vertically upward and bounced off a warm layer in the atmosphere, returning to spread across the surface at a distance of about 80 miles (130 km) wide around the volcano, leaving a ring of silence within the danger zone of the eruption. Some of the sound of the eruption near the blast may also have been absorbed by the huge amounts of ash in the air.

Loss of the weight from the bulge released pressure on the magma inside the volcano, and the side of the mountain exploded outward at 300 MPH (500 km/hr). The preexisting rock mixed with magma and rose to temperatures of 200°F (93°C). This mass flew into Spirit Lake on the northern flank of the volcano and formed a wave 650 feet (200 m) high that destroyed much of the landscape. Lahars filled the north and south forks of the Toutle River, Pine Creek, and Muddy River. Some of these lahars included masses of ash, mud, and debris, filling much of the Toutle River to a depth of 150 feet (50 m) and locally to as deep as 600 feet (180 m). As the mudflows moved downhill and away from the volcano they became mixed with more water from the streams and picked up speed. This prompted a mass evacuation of areas downhill from the volcano, saving countless lives. Vehicles and more than 200 homes were swept away, bridges knocked out, and the lumber industry devastated.

A hot pyroclastic flow blasted out of the hole on the side of the volcano and moved at 250 MPH (400 km/hr), knocking over and burying trees and everything in its path for hundreds of square miles. The USGS observation post was destroyed, killing the geologist manning the equipment. The forests were a scene of utter devastation after the blast; trees up to 20 feet (6 m) in diameter were snapped at their bases and blown down for miles around, destroying an estimated 3.7 billion board feet of timber. The blast moved so fast that it jumped over ramps in the slope, knocking down trees on the side of a knob facing the volcano, while leaving standing charred remains of the trees that were in the blast shadow hidden behind cliffs on the downwind sides of hills. The wildlife in the forest was virtually wiped out, but began to return within a couple of years of the eruption. Remarkably, some of the wildlife that lived underground in burrows or beneath lakes and rocks survived, so some of these resilient beavers, frogs, salamanders, crayfish, as well as some flowers, shrubs, and small trees served to help regenerate the ecological systems in the eruption zone.

A huge Plinian ash cloud that erupted to heights of 12 miles (25 km) placed a half-billion tons of volcanic ash and debris into the atmosphere. This ash was carried by winds and dropped over much of the western United States. Pyroclastic flows continued to move down the volcano at a rate of 60 MPH (96 km/hr) and temperatures of 550–700°F (288–370°C). Sixty-two people died in this relatively minor eruption and damage to property is estimated to have been $1 billion. Volcanic ash fell like heavy black rain across much of eastern Washington, Idaho, and Montana. Finer-grained ash that made it into the upper atmosphere managed to circle the globe within 17 days and created spectacular sunsets for months. Even though the amount of ash that fell was relatively minor compared to some other historical eruptions, the ash caused major problems throughout the Pacific Northwest. Planes were grounded, many electrical transformers short-circuited, and mechanical engines and motor vehicles became inoperable, stranding thousands of people. Breathing was difficult and many people had to wear face masks. Rains came and turned the ash layers into a terrible mud that became like concrete, resting heavily on buildings and collapsing roofs.

Smaller eruptions and pyroclastic flows continued to move down the mountain less and less frequently over the next two years, as a new resurgent dome began to grow in the crater created by the blast that

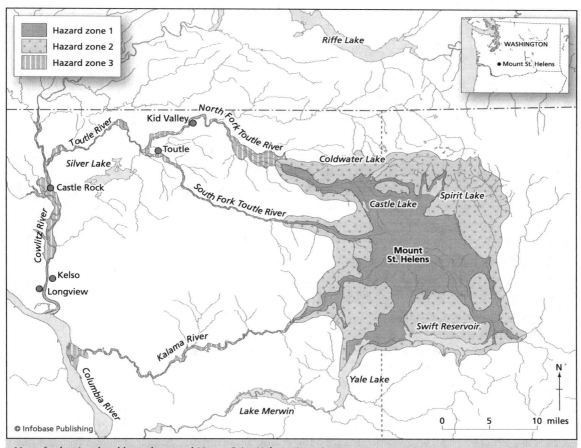

Map of volcanic-related hazards around Mount Saint Helens *(USGS)*

removed the top of the mountain. As the dome grows, residents wait for the next eruption of a Cascades volcano.

Mount Pinatubo, 1991

The eruption of Mount Pinatubo in the Philippines in 1991 was the second largest volcanic eruption of the 20th century (after Katmai in Alaska in 1912) and offers many lessons in volcanic prediction, warning, evacuation, and resettlement that may serve as blueprints for future eruptions around the world. Pinatubo offers reassuring evidence that careful volcanic monitoring can lead to public warnings and evacuations that can save thousands of lives during catastrophic volcanic eruptions.

Mount Pinatubo is located on the Philippine island of Luzon, about 50 miles (80 km) northwest of Manila and close to what was U.S. Clark Air Base. Prior to 1991, Mount Pinatubo was known to be a volcano but was not thought to pose much of a threat since it had not erupted for approximately 500 years. Almost half a million people lived on or near the volcano, including about 16,000 Americans stationed at Clark Air Base. As soon as Pinatubo began to show signs of activity, Philippine and USGS personnel set up volcano-monitoring stations and equipment, providing detailed and constantly updated evaluations of the status of the volcano and the potential danger levels and likelihood of an impending eruption. Geologists coordinated efforts with local military, civil defense, and disaster planning officials and quickly worked on determining the volcanic history and mapping areas most at risk. Critically important was examining the past eruption history to determine how violent past eruptions had been, as an indicator about how bad any impending eruption could be. What the geologists found was frightening, as they determined that Pinatubo had a history of producing tremendous and extremely explosive eruptions and that such an event might be in the making for the period of activity they were examining. They didn't have long to wait to realize their fears.

Precursors to the giant eruption of Pinatubo in June 1991 may have been initiated by a large earthquake on July 16, 1990, centered about 60 miles (100 km) northeast of Pinatubo. This earthquake may have somehow started a series of events that allowed magma to rise beneath the volcano, perhaps opening cracks and fissures beneath it. Soon after this, local villagers (the Aetas, a seminomadic people who had lived on the volcano for about 400 years, ever since fleeing to the area to hide from Spaniards) reported activity on the mountain, including low rumbling sounds, landslides near the summit, and steam eruptions from fissures.

Seismologists were able to measure five small earthquakes around Pinatubo in the next several weeks, but then activity seemed to quiet down for six months.

The first major steam eruption from Pinatubo was observed by villagers, who reported a 1-mile-long (1.6-km-) fissure exploding and emitting ash from the north side of the volcano on April 2, 1991. Ash covered surrounding villages, and the Philippine Institute of Volcanology & Seismology (PHIVOLCS) and military and civil defense authorities set up a series of seismographs around the volcano, which promptly recorded more than 200 earthquakes the next day. Authorities declared a volcanic emergency, recommending that villagers within 6 miles (10 km) of the summit be evacuated. Volcano experts from the USGS joined the observation and monitoring team on April 23, bringing a plethora of monitoring equipment with them. The local and American teams set up a joint volcano monitoring observatory, the Pinatubo Volcano Observatory, at Clark Air Base, where they also monitored seven seismic stations placed around the volcano.

By the middle of May, the Pinatubo Volcano Observatory was recording 30 to 180 earthquakes a day, at the same time that geologists were scrambling to complete fieldwork to understand the past eruptive behavior of the mountain. The geologists were able to determine that the volcanic basement to the modern peak was about 1 million years old and the mountain itself had been built by around six major violent eruptions in the past 35,000 years. They determined that the eruptions were becoming slightly less violent with time, but more frequent, with the last major eruption about 500 years ago. The mountain was overdue for a large violent eruption.

On May 13, volcanologists measured emissions of sulfur dioxide gas, an indicator that magma at depth was rising beneath the volcano. In consultation with the volcano observatory scientists, civil defense authorities issued a series of levels of alerts that they could use to warn the public in the event of a catastrophic eruption. These alert levels were updated several times per day, and geologists published new hazard maps showing locations where mudflows, lahars, ashfalls, and nuée ardents were most likely to occur during an eruption.

Thousands of small earthquakes and greater amounts of sulfur dioxide indicated that magma was still rising beneath the volcano in May, with estimates showing that the magma had risen to within 1.2–4 miles (2–6 km) beneath the surface of the volcano. It was difficult to interpret the warning signs of the impending eruption and to determine if and when it might occur. The geologists and government officials were torn between ordering immediate evacuations and perhaps saving hundreds of thousands of lives or letting villagers stay until the danger grew more imminent and letting them harvest their fields.

On June 1, many of the earthquakes became concentrated in one area beneath a steam vent on the northwest side of the summit, which began to bulge outward. On June 3, the volcano began to spew a series of ash eruptions, which continued to increase so that the volcanic alert level was raised to level 3 (meaning an eruption was possible within two weeks). About 10,000 villagers were evacuated, and, on June 7, the volcano had a minor eruption that sent ash and steam to a height of about 5 miles (8 km) above the summit. The volcano was bulging more, and there were more than 1,500 earthquakes per day, prompting the alert level to be raised to level 4 (eruption possible within 24 hours) and the evacuation zone to be doubled in distance from the volcano.

June 7 saw a small magma dome oozing out of the volcano about half a mile northwest of the peak of the volcano, the first sign that magma had reached the surface. Two days later, large amounts of sulfur dioxide began to escape again (after stopping for several weeks), and small nuée ardents began to tumble down the slopes of the volcano. The volcanic alert was raised to level 5 (eruption in progress) and massive evacu-

Mount Pinatubo, Philippines, June 1991. First major eruption of Mount Pinatubo, viewed from Clark Air Base *(R. S. Culbreth, USGS)*

Mount Pinatubo, Philippines. View of World Airways DC-10 airplane sitting on its tail because of weight of June 15, 1991, ash *(R. L. Rieger, Cubi Point Naval Air Station)*

ations began. The ash eruptions grew larger, and, on June 10, all aircraft and 14,500 U.S. personnel from Clark Air Base left for safer ground at nearby Subic Bay Naval Base, leaving only 1,500 American personnel and three helicopters at Clark.

At 8:51 A.M. on June 12, the mountain sent huge columns of hot ash surging 12 miles (20 km) high in the atmosphere, spawning nuée ardents that covered some now-evacuated villages. Skies became dark, and everything for miles around began to be covered with ash. The evacuation radius was increased to 18 miles (30 km) from the volcano, with the numbers of evacuated now approximately 73,000. Eruptions continued, and, on June 13, another huge explosion sent ash past 15 miles (25 km) into the atmosphere. Then the volcano became ominously quiet.

Another large eruption broke the silence at 1:09 P.M., followed quickly by a series of 13 more blasts over the next day. Nuée ardents roared through several more evacuated villages, burying them in hot ash, while typhoon Yunya pelted the area and added wind and rain to the ash, making a miserable mixture. Ash covered the entire region, thousands of square miles, with a layer of heavy wet ash-muck. Ash and pumice began falling heavily on Clark Air Base, and the remaining staff from the observatory fled to a nearby college.

As they were leaving, the eruption style changed dramatically for the worse, rapidly moving into the realm of giant eruptions and becoming the second largest eruption in the world in the 20th century. The cataclysmic eruption continued for more than nine hours and more than 90 percent of the material erupted was blasted into the air. Huge billowing Plinian ash columns rose more than 21 miles (34 km) and spread across 250 square miles (1,000 sq km). The top of the volcano began to collapse into the empty magma chamber, prompting fears of a truly catastrophic eruption that luckily proved unfounded. The magma was largely drained, and the top of the volcano collapsed into empty space forming a large caldera whose summit lies 870 feet (265 m) below the volcano's former height of 5,724 feet (1745 m). Ash, nuée ardent, and lahar deposits hundreds of feet thick filled the valleys draining the flanks of Pinatubo, and thick ash covered buildings across an area of more than 210,000 square miles (340,000 sq km). Approximately 5–6 cubic miles (20–25 cubic km) of volcanic material was blasted from Pinatubo, along with more than 17 megatons of sulfur dioxide, 3–16 megatons of chlorine and 420,234 megatons of carbon dioxide.

The devastation was remarkable, with buildings wiped away by nuée ardents and mudflows or collapsed from the weight of wet ash on their roofs. Crops were destroyed and roads and canals made impassable. Ash covered much of Luzon and fell across the South China Sea and remained in the atmosphere for more than a year. Smaller eruptions continued, decreasing in frequency throughout July to about one per day by the end of August, stopping completely on September 4. Soon after, a new lava dome rose in the caldera in July 1992, but no large eruption ensued. Only between 200 to 300 people died in the initial eruption, although more were to die later in mudflows and other events, bringing the total deaths to 1,202. Most of the initial deaths were of people who took shelter in buildings whose roofs collapsed under the weight of the rain-soaked volcanic ash.

Atmospheric effects of Pinatubo are well documented and clearly show the climatic effects of large volcanic eruptions. The gas cloud from Pinatubo formed from the combination of ash, water, and sulfur dioxide and was the largest cloud of sulfuric acid aerosol since that produced by Krakatau in 1883. This sulfuric acid aerosol eventually reached the ozone layer where it destroyed huge quantities of ozone and greatly increased the size of the ozone hole over Antarctica. It took only three weeks for the sulfuric acid cloud to spread around the world between 10°S and 30°N latitudes, dropping global temperatures from one-half to one degree and causing spectacular sunsets. The cloud remained detectable in the atmosphere until the end of 1993. Many unusual weather patterns have been attributed to the global lowering of temperatures by the Pinatubo cloud, including colder, wetter, and stormier winters in many locations.

Most of the evacuated villagers lost livestock, homes, and crops, but survived because of the well-timed warnings and prompt and responsible evacuations by government officials. However, conditions in the refugee camps were not ideal and about 350 additional people died after the eruption from measles, diarrhea, and respiratory infections. The rainy season was approaching, and many mudflows began sweeping down the flanks of the volcano at 20 MPH (30 km/hr), spreading across once-lush farmland. Hundreds of mudflows were recorded on the eastern flank of the volcano in the last few (rainy) months of 1993, killing another 100 people. Mudflow warning systems and alert levels were set up, saving many additional lives in coming years.

Economic losses from the eruption of Pinatubo were tremendous, stunting the economy of the Philippines. Damage to crops and property amounted to $443 million by 1992, with another $100 million spent on refugees and another $150 million on mudflow controls. Eight thousand homes were destroyed and 650,000 people lost jobs for at least several months. The U.S. air and naval bases at Clark and Subic Bay closed, leading to additional job losses in the region.

Mount Pinatubo provided valuable information to geologists and atmospheric scientists about the amount of and types of volcanic gases injected into the atmosphere during volcanic eruptions and the effects these gases have on climate and the environment. Most gases in the atmosphere are volcanic in origin, so volcanoes have had a direct link to climate and human activities over geologic time. The relative importance of release of volcanic gases by volcanoes versus the emission of greenhouse gases by humans in climate change is currently a hotly debated topic. If volcanoes can produce more aerosols and gases in a few days or weeks than humans produce in years, then volcanic eruptions may drastically change the rates of climate change that are produced by natural cycles and human-related emissions.

Gases released from Mount Pinatubo produced an average global cooling around the planet, yet also were associated with winter warming over the Northern Hemisphere for two years following the eruption. These unexpected effects resulted from complex differences in the way the aerosols were distributed in the stratosphere. Aerosol heating in the lower stratosphere combined with a depletion of ozone to contribute to local warming in the Northern Hemisphere winters. The average atmospheric cooling has also been implicated in some biological responses to the volcanic eruption. Coral reefs are very sensitive to small variations in temperature, and, after the eruption of Pinatubo, coral reefs in the Red Sea saw a massive die-off that was probably related to the atmospheric cooling. The gases in the atmosphere also caused incoming solar radiation to be more diffuse, which led to greater vegetation growth. These additional plants in turn drew a greater amount of carbon dioxide out of the atmosphere, further cooling the planet. It has also been hypothesized that Northern Hemisphere winter warming led to a spike in the number of polar bear cubs born the following spring. Most observations and models for atmospheric evolution following massive eruptions show that the aerosol and ozone levels recover to pre-eruption levels within 5 to 10 years after the eruption.

Nyiragongo, Congo, 2002

Nyiragongo volcano is located in Congo (formerly Zaire) in the East African rift valley, along an extensional plate boundary. Nyiragongo is an 11,380-foot- (3,469-m-) tall stratovolcano cone that has experienced significant eruptions, including one in 1977 that killed 70 people. It is one of the most active volcanoes along the East African rift valley and contained a lava lake in its crater from 1894 through 1977. Another lava lake formed in 1982 before the 2002 eruption. Nyiragongo entered a new active eruption period in January 2002, sending blocky lava flows into the town of Goma on the shores of Lake Kivu. Lava flows six feet (2 m) deep covered much of the town, burning buildings, crops, blocking streets, and sending 300,000 people fleeing across the border into Rwanda. In some places, the lava moved so quickly, at speeds of up to 40 MPH (60 km/hr), that people could barely outrun it. The lava ignited fuel tanks and gasoline stations, causing many explosions and fires. People who were trying to siphon gas out of an aboveground tank for personal use initiated one particularly large explosion. Somebody accidentally dropped a bottle of gasoline on the hot lava (estimated to be 1,858°F [1,000°C] just below a thin surface crust), setting off a massive fireball in which several dozen people died. Nearly three-quarters of Goma was destroyed in the eruption.

Conclusion

Comparison of historical accounts of ancient eruptions with high-technology observations of modern volcanic eruptions shows that it is possible to predict, with varying degrees of accuracy, many of the processes that have led to loss of life during volcanic eruptions. Large volcanic eruptions typically are preceded by periods of earthquakes, small eruptions, emissions of gas, and other phenomena that can be monitored, and authorities can work with scientists to know when to best alert the public that it is time to evacuate the areas closest to a volcano to save their lives. The successful prediction of the massive eruption of Mount Pinatubo in the Philippines in 1990 undoubtedly saved thousands of lives, and many lessons can be learned from examining the coordination of scientific, civilian, and military officials in evacuating the public. There is often a fine line to draw between deciding when to call for a low level volcanic alert, in which tens of thousands of people need not leave their homes, farms, livelihoods, and villages at great loss of income and convenience, and when to call for a massive evacuation to save the lives of those in the path of a potentially killer volcano.

6

Massive Global Volcanism, Volcanic Winters, and Kimberlite Eruptions

Some volcanic events are either so large in scale or so violent that they are outside the scope of normal volcanic activity. Some massive global volcanic events have occurred where the total volume of magma erupted in any period is triple or even 10 times the normal amounts, and in other cases individual volcanic provinces have produced as much magma as the rest of the planet combined. These types of massive volcanic events also place large amounts of carbon dioxide into the atmosphere and in this way influence global climate.

Some volcanic events occur so suddenly, with a supersonic blast from deep in the Earth, that they are classified separately from other types of volcanic activity. Kimberlite explosions are where magma from Earth's mantle suddenly explodes at the surface, sending plumes high into the atmosphere. These explosions leave vertical pipes behind, sometimes filled with diamond-bearing ultramafic rocks brought up from 100 miles (160 km) deep within the Earth.

Massive Global Volcanic Events

At several times in Earth's history, vast outpourings of lava have accumulated, forming thick piles of basalt, representing the largest-known volcanic episodes on the planet in the past several hundred million years. These deposits include continental *flood basalt* provinces, anomalously thick and topographically high seafloor known as oceanic plateaus and some volcanic rifted *passive margins*. These piles of volcanic rock represent times when the Earth moved more material and energy from its interior in extremely short time periods than during the entire intervals between the massive volcanic events. Such large amounts of volcanism also released large amounts of volcanic gases into the atmosphere, with serious implications for global temperatures and climate and may have contributed to some global *mass extinctions.* Many are associated with periods of global cooling where volcanic gases reduce the amount of incoming solar radiation, resulting in volcanic winters.

The largest continental flood basalt province in the United States is the Columbia River flood basalt in Washington, Oregon, and Idaho. The Columbia River flood basalt province is 6–17 million years old and contains an estimated 1,250 cubic miles (5,210 cubic km) of basalt. Individual lava flows erupted through fissures or cracks in the crust, then flowed laterally across the plain for up to 400 miles (640 km).

The 66-million-year-old Deccan flood basalts, also known as traps, cover a large part of western India and the Seychelles. They are associated with the breakup of India from the Seychelles during the opening of the Indian Ocean. Slightly older flood basalts (90–83 million years old) are associated with the breaking away of Madagascar from India. The volume of the Deccan traps is estimated at 5,000,000 cubic miles (20,840,000 cubic km), and the volcanics are thought to have been erupted in about 1 million years, starting slightly before the great Cretaceous-Tertiary extinction 66 million years ago. Most people now agree that the gases released during this period of flood basalt volcanism stressed the global biosphere to such an extent that many marine organisms were forced into extinction and many others were stressed. Then the planet was hit by the meteorite that formed the massive Chicxulub impact crater on the Yucatán Peninsula (Mexico), causing massive extinction including the end of the dinosaurs.

The breakup of East Africa along the East African rift system and the Red Sea is associated with large amounts of Cenozoic (less than 30 million years old) continental flood basalts. Some of the older volcanic fields are located in East Africa in the Afar region of Ethiopia, south into Kenya and Uganda, and north across the Red Sea and Gulf of Aden into Yemen and Saudi Arabia. These volcanic piles are overlain by younger (less than 15 million years old) flood basalts that extend both farther south into Tanzania and farther north through central Arabia, where they are known as Harrats, and into Syria, Israel, Lebanon, and Jordan.

An older volcanic province also associated with the breakup of a continent is known as the North Atlantic Igneous Province. It formed along with the breakup of the North Atlantic Ocean 62 to 55 million years ago and includes both onshore and offshore volcanic flows and intrusions in Greenland, Iceland, and the northern British Isles, including most of the Rockall Plateau and Faeroe Islands. In the southern Atlantic, a similar 129–134–million-year-old flood basalt was split by the opening of the ocean and now has two parts. In Brazil, the flood lavas are known as the Paraná basalts and, in Namibia and Angola, as the Etendeka basalts.

The Caribbean ocean floor represents one of the best examples of an oceanic plateau, with other major examples including the Ontong-Java Plateau, Manihiki Plateau, Hess Rise, Shatsky Rise, and Mid-Pacific Mountains. All of these oceanic plateaus contain 6–25-mile- (40-km-) thick piles of volcanic and subvolcanic rocks representing huge outpourings of lava. The Caribbean seafloor preserves 5–13-mile- (8–21-km-) thick oceanic crust formed about 85 million years ago in the eastern Pacific Ocean. This unusually thick floor was transported eastward by plate tectonics, where pieces of the seafloor collided with South America as it passed into the Atlantic Ocean. Pieces of the Caribbean oceanic crust are now preserved in Colombia, Ecuador, Panama, Hispaniola, and Cuba, and some scientists estimate that the Caribbean oceanic plateau may once have been twice its present size. In any case, it represents a vast outpouring of lava that would have been associated with significant outgassing with possible consequences for global climate and evolution.

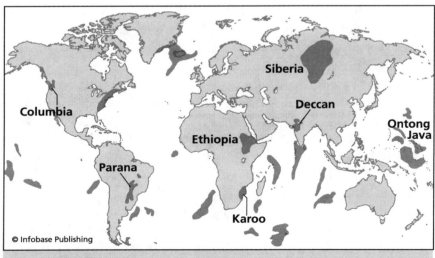

Map of flood basalts on the planet

The western Pacific Ocean basin contains several large oceanic plateaus, including the 20-mile- (32-km-) thick crust of the Alaska-sized Ontong-Java Plateau, which is the largest outpouring of volcanic rocks on the planet. It apparently formed in two intervals, at 122 and 90 million years ago, entirely within the ocean, and represents magma that rose in a plume from deep in the mantle and erupted on the seafloor. It is estimated that the volume of magma erupted in the first event was equivalent to that of all the magma being erupted at mid-ocean ridges at the present time. Sea levels rose by more than 30 feet (9 m) in response to this volcanic outpouring. The gases released during these eruptions are estimated to have raised average global temperatures by 23°F (13°C).

Environmental Hazards of Flood Basalt Volcanism

The environmental impact of the eruption of large volumes of basalt in provinces including those described above can be severe. Huge volumes of sulfur dioxide, carbon dioxide, chlorine, and flourine are released during large basaltic eruptions. Much of this gas may get injected into the upper troposphere and lower stratosphere during the eruption process, being released from eruption columns that reach 2–8 miles (3–13 km) in height. Carbon dioxide is a greenhouse gas and can cause global warming, whereas sulfur dioxide and hydrogen sulfate have the opposite effect and can cause short-term cooling. Many of the episodes of volcanism preserved in these large igneous provinces were rapid, repeatedly releasing enormous quantities of gases over periods of less than one million years, enough to significantly change the climate more rapidly than organisms could adapt. For instance, one eruption of the Columbia River basalts is estimated to have released 9,000 million tons (8,860 tonnes) of sulfur dioxide and thousands of millions of tons of other gases, whereas the eruption of Mount Pinatubo in 1991 released about 20 million tons (19.7 tonnes) of sulfur dioxide.

The Columbia River basalts of the Pacific Northwest continued erupting for years at a time for approximately 1 million years. During this time, the gases released would be equivalent to that of Mount Pinatubo every week, over periods maintained for decades to thousands of years at a time. The atmospheric consequences are sobering. Sulfuric acid aerosols and acid from the flourine and chlorine would form extensive poisonous acid rain, destroying habitats and making waters uninhabitable for some organisms. At the very least, the environmental consequences would be such that organisms were stressed to the point that they would not be able to handle an additional environmental stress, such as a global volcanic winter and subsequent warming caused by a giant impact.

Faunal extinctions have been correlated with the eruption of the Deccan flood basalts at the Cretaceous-Tertiary boundary and with the Siberian flood basalts at the Permian-Triassic boundary. There is still considerable debate about the relative significance of flood basalt volcanism and impacts of meteorites for extinction events, particularly at the Cretaceous-Tertiary boundary. Some geologists suggest that the extinction was due entirely to an impact, whereas others suggest that there was no impact and that volcanism can explain all of the environmental changes that led to extinction. However, most scientists would now agree that the global environment was stressed shortly before the Cretaceous-Tertiary boundary by volcanic-induced climate change and then a huge meteorite hit the Yucatán Peninsula, forming the Chicxulub impact crater, causing the massive Cretaceous-Tertiary boundary extinction and the death of the dinosaurs.

The Siberian flood basalts cover a large area of the Central Siberian Plateau northwest of Lake Baikal. They are more than half a mile thick over an area of 210,000 square miles (543,900 sq km), but have been significantly eroded from an estimated volume of 1,240,000 cubic miles (3,211,600 cubic km). They were erupted over an extraordinarily short period of less than 1 million years 250 million years ago at the Permian-Triassic boundary. They are remarkably coincident in time with the major Permian/Triassic extinction, implying a causal link. The Permian/Triassic boundary at 250 million years ago marks the greatest extinction in Earth's history, where 90 percent of marine species and 70 percent of terrestrial vertebrates became extinct. It has been postulated that rapid volcanism and degassing released enough sulfur dioxide to cause a rapid global cooling, inducing a short ice age with associated rapid fall of sea level. Soon after the ice age took hold, the effects of the carbon dioxide took over and the atmosphere heated, resulting in a global warming. The rapidly fluctuating climate postulated to have been caused by the volcanic gases is thought to have killed off many organisms, which were simply unable to cope with the wildly fluctuating climate extremes.

Kimberlites and Diatremes

Kimberlites and diatremes represent rare types of continental volcanic rock, produced by generally explosive volcanism with an origin deep within the mantle. They form pipelike bodies extending vertically downward and are the source of most of the world's diamonds. Kimberlites were first discovered in South Africa during diamond exploration and mining in 1869, when the source of many alluvial diamonds on the Vaal, Orange, and Riet Rivers was found to be circular mud "pans," later appreciated to be kimberlite pipes. In 1871, two very diamond-rich kimberlite pipes were discovered on the Vooruitzigt Farm, owned by Nicolas de Beer. These discoveries led to the establishment of several large mines and one of the most influential mining companies in history.

Kimberlites are very complicated volcanic rocks with mixtures of material derived from the upper mantle and complex water-rich magma of several different varieties. A range of volcanic intrusive styles, including some extremely explosive events, characterizes kimberlites. True volcanic lavas are only rarely associated with kimberlites, so volcanic styles of typical volcanoes are not typical of kimberlites. Most near-surface kimberlite rocks are pyroclastic deposits formed by explosive volcanism filling vertical pipes and surrounded by rings of volcanic tuff and related features. The pipes are typically a couple hundred yards wide, with the tuff ring extending another hundred yards or so beyond the pipes. The very upper part of many kimberlite pipes includes reworked pyroclastic rocks, deposited in lakes that filled the kimberlite pipes after the explosive volcanism blasted much of the kimberlite material out of the hole. Geologic studies of kimberlites have suggested that they intrude the crust suddenly and behave differently from typical volcanoes. Kimberlites intrude violently and catastrophically, with the initial formation of a pipe filled with brecciated material from the mantle, reflecting the sudden and explosive character of the eruption. As the eruption wanes, a series of tuffs fall out of the eruption column and deposit the tuff ring around the pipes. Unlike most volcanoes, kimberlite eruptions are not followed by the intrusion of magma into the pipe. The pipes simply get eroded by near-surface processes, lakes form in the pipes, and nature tries to hide the very occurrence of the explosive event.

Below these upward-expanding craters are deep vertical pipes known as diatremes that extend down into the mantle, source region of the kimberlites. Many diatremes have features that suggest the brecciated mantle and crustal rocks were emplaced at low temperature, nonviolently, presenting a great puzzle to geologists. How can a deep source of broken mantle rocks passively move up a vertical pipe to the surface, suddenly explode violently, and then disappear beneath a newly formed lake?

DIAMONDS AND KIMBERLITES

Diamonds are stable crystalline forms of pure carbon that only form at high pressures in cool locations in the Earth's mantle and thus are restricted in their origin to places in the subcontinental mantle where these conditions exist, between 90–125 miles (150–200 km) depth. The vast majority of diamonds that make their way back to the surface are brought up from these great depths by rare explosive volcanic eruptions known as kimberlites.

Diamonds are the hardest substance known and widely used as a gemstone. Uncut varieties may show many different crystal shapes and many show striated crystal faces. They crystallize in isometric tetrahedral forms, have concoidal fracture, have a greasy luster, and may be clear, yellow, red, orange, green, blue, brown, or even black. Triangular depressions are common on some crystals, and others may form elongate or even pear-shaped forms. Diamonds have been found in alluvial deposits such as gravel, and some mines have been located by tracing the source of the gravel back to the kimberlite pipe where the diamonds were brought to the surface. Some diamond-mining operations such as those of the Vaal River, South Africa (discovered in 1867), proceeded for many years before it was recognized that the source was in nearby kimberlites.

Dating the age of formation of small mineral inclusions in diamonds has yielded some very important results. All diamonds from the mantle appear to be Precambrian in age, with one type being up to 3.2 billion years old and another 1.0–1.6 billion years old. Since diamonds form at high pressures and low temperatures, their very existence shows that the temperature deep in the Earth beneath the continents in the Precambrian was not much hotter than it is today. The diamonds were stored deep beneath the continents for billions of years before being erupted in the kimberlite pipes.

Early ideas for the intrusion and surface explosion of kimberlites suggested that they rose explosively and catastrophically from their origin in the mantle. Subsequent studies revealed that the early deep parts of their ascent did not seem to be explosive. It is likely that kimberlite magma rises from deep in the upper mantle along a series of cracks and fissures until it gets to shallow levels where it mixes with water and becomes extremely explosive. Other diatremes may be more explosive from greater depths and may move as gas-filled bodies rising from the upper mantle. As the gases move into lower pressure areas they would expand, resulting in the kimberlite moving faster until it explodes at the surface. Still other ideas for the emplacement of kimberlites and diatremes invoke hydrovolcanism, or the interaction of the deep magma with near-surface water. Magma may rise slowly from depth until it encounters ground-

Kimberlite pipe outside of Mirney, Russia. Diamonds are formed in the Earth's mantle and brought up to the surface in the volcanic rock called kimberlite. Kimberlites form pipe-shaped intrusions, and diamond miners dig vertically downward, following the pipe into the Earth. *(Sergei Karpukhin, Reuters/Landov)*

water in fractures or other voids, then explode when the water mixes with the magma. The resulting explosion could produce the volcanic features and upward expanding pipe found in many kimberlites.

It is likely that some or all of the processes discussed here play a role in the intrusion of kimberlites and diatremes, the important consequence being a sudden, explosive volcanic eruption at the surface, far from typical locations of volcanism, and the relatively rapid removal of signs of this volcanism. The initial explosions are likely to be so explosive that they may blast material to the stratosphere, though other kimberlite eruptions may only form small eruptions and ash clouds. The hazards are thus similar to other volcanic hazards, but the location of kimberlites is more likely to be in the middle of a stable continental region.

Conclusion

Flood basalts and kimberlites represent two unusual types of volcanism that fortunately have not erupted on the surface in recent history. Volcanic flows from these eruptions have covered hundreds of thousands to millions of square miles. The massive amounts of volcanism preserved in flood basalt provinces such as the Columbia River basalts of the Pacific Northwest have poured out atmospheric gases equivalent to that of Mount Pinatubo each year, for thousands of years. The climate effects of these types of huge eruptions are enormous, lowering global temperatures and contributing to the formation of ice ages and global mass extinction events. Kimberlites are extremely rare types of volcanic events where diamond-bearing material moves up from the mantle and suddenly explodes at the surface, with such force that the explosion blows a hole through the atmosphere. After the explosion the volcanic event is over, and the explosion pipe is typically rapidly eroded to form a lake or buried under younger deposits.

7

Mass Extinctions and Catastrophes

Most of the volcanic disasters discussed in this book have been about events that have resulted in tremendous loss of life and property, with death tolls in the thousands to hundreds of thousands of people in some cases, and, in a few examples, with indirect death tolls reaching into the millions on a global scale. While these disasters have been catastrophic and every effort should be taken to prevent such disasters from occurring, the Earth has experienced several major events that makes all of these catastrophes pale in comparison. The previous chapter touched on the relationship between mass extinctions and the global effects of massive volcanism. In this chapter, mass extinctions are examined in more detail, since they represent the largest and most significant natural disasters in the history of the Earth, and many models suggest that massive global volcanic events may contribute to mass extinction events. Understanding mass extinctions may some day save the human race from the same fate.

Geologists and paleontologists study the history of life on Earth through detailed examination of that record as preserved in sedimentary rock layers. For hundreds of years, paleontologists have recognized that many organisms are found in a series of layers and then suddenly disappear at a certain horizon never to reappear in the succeeding progressively younger layers. These disappearances have been interpreted to mark extinctions of the organisms from the biosphere. After hundreds of years of work, many of these rock layers have been dated by using radioactive decay dating techniques on volcanic rocks in the sequences, and many of these sedimentary rock sequences have been correlated with each other on a global scale.

One of the more important results that have come from such detailed studies is that the rock record preserves a record of several extinction events that have occurred simultaneously on a global scale. Furthermore, these events do not just affect thousands or hundreds of thousands of members of a species, but they have wiped out many species and families each containing millions or billions of individuals.

The Role of Non-Catastrophic Processes in Evolution and Extinction

Several processes may strongly influence the progression of life, evolution, and extinction on Earth. Variations in the style of plate tectonics or the positions of the continents, massive global volcanic events, and continental collisions can all affect life, evolution, and extinction. Plate tectonics and massive volcanic events also may cause glaciation and climate changes, which in turn influence evolution and extinction.

One of the primary ways that normal, non-catastrophic plate tectonic mechanisms drive evolution and extinction is through tectonic-induced changes to sea level. Fluctuating sea levels cause the global climate to fluctuate between warm periods when shallow seas are easily heated and cold periods when glaciation draws the water down and displaces shorelines so that they are located along the steep continental slopes. Many species cannot tolerate such variations in temperature and drastic changes to their shallow shelf environments and thus become extinct. After organisms from a specific environment die off, their environmental niches are available for other species to inhabit.

Sea levels have risen and fallen dramatically in Earth's history, with water covering all but 5 percent of the land surface at times and water falling so that continents occupy 40 percent more of the planet's surface than at other times. The most important plate tectonic mechanism of changing sea level is to change the average depth of the seafloor by changing the volume of the mid-ocean ridge system through dramatic changes in the amount of seafloor volcanism. If the undersea ridges take up more space in the ocean basins, then the water will be displaced higher onto the land, much like dropping pebbles into a birdbath may cause it to overflow. In this way, volcanism is related to sea levels, which is related to biological evolution. Increases or decreases in the amount of seafloor volcanism also dramatically change the amount of gases released to the atmosphere.

How can the volume of the mid-ocean ridge system be changed? There are several mechanisms, all of which may have the same effect. Young oceanic crust is hotter, more buoyant, and topographically higher than older crust. If the average age of the oceanic crust is decreased then more of the crust will be at shallow depths, displacing more water onto the continents. If seafloor spreading rates are increased then the average age of oceanic crust will be decreased, the volume of the ridges will be increased through increased volcanic activity, the average age of the seafloor will be decreased, and sea levels will rise. This has happened at several times in Earth's history, including during the mid-Cretaceous when sea levels were 660 feet (200 m) higher than they are today, covering much of the central United States and other low-lying continents with water. This also warmed global climates, because the sun easily warmed the abundant shallow seas. It has also been suggested that sea levels were consistently much higher in the Precambrian, when seafloor spreading rates were likely to have been generally faster.

Sea levels can also rise from additional magmatism on the seafloor. If the Earth goes through a period where seafloor volcanoes erupt more magma on the seafloor, then the space occupied by these volcanic deposits will be displaced onto the continents. The additional volcanic rocks may be erupted at hot spot volcanoes such as in Hawaii or along the mid-ocean ridge system, either way the result is the same. An increased amount of volcanic rocks on the sea will displace the water that formerly occupied this space onto higher levels on the continents.

Simply having more mid-ocean ridges on the seafloor may increase sea level height by increasing the volume of ridges that displace seawater. At the present time, the mid-ocean ridge system is 40,000 miles (65,000 km) long. If the Earth goes through a period where it needs to lose more heat, such as in the Precambrian, one of the ways it may do this is by increasing the length of the ridge system where magmas erupt and lose heat to the seawater. If the total ridge length is doubled, then the globally averaged amount of volcanism will also roughly double. Ridge lengths were probably greater early in Earth's history in the Precambrian, which together with faster seafloor spreading and increased magmatism may have kept sea levels at high levels for millions of years.

Sea level may also be changed by glaciation, which may be induced by tectonic or astronomical causes. At present, glaciers cover much of Antarctica, Greenland, and mountain ranges in several regions. There are approximately 6 million cubic miles (25,000,000 cubic km) of ice locked up in glaciers. If this ice were to all melt, then sea levels would rise by 230 feet (70 m), covering many coastal regions, cities, and interior farmland with shallow seas. During the last glacial maximum in the Pleistocene ice ages (20,000 years ago), sea levels were 460 feet (140 m) lower than today, with shorelines up to hundreds of miles seaward of their present locations, along the continental slopes.

Continental collisions and especially the formation of *supercontinents* can cause glaciations. When continents collide, many of the carbonate rocks deposited on continental shelves is exposed to weathering. As the carbonates and other minerals weather, their weathering products react with atmospheric elements and tend to combine with atmospheric carbon dioxide. Carbon dioxide is a greenhouse gas that keeps the climate warm, and steady reductions of it in the atmosphere by weathering or other processes lowers global temperatures. Thus, times of continental collision and supercontinent formation tend to be times that draw carbon dioxide out of the atmosphere, plunging the Earth into a cold icehouse period. In the cases of supercontinent formation, this icehouse may remain in effect until the supercontinent breaks up and massive amounts of seafloor volcanism associated with new rifts and ridges add new carbon dioxide back into the atmosphere.

The formation and dispersal of supercontinent fragments and migrating landmasses in general also strongly influence evolution and extinction. When supercontinents break up, a large amount of shallow continental shelf area is created. Life-forms tend to flourish in the diverse environments on the continental shelves, and many spurts in evolution have occurred in the shallow shelf areas. In contrast, when continental areas are isolated, such as Australia and Madagascar today, life-forms evolve independently. If plate tectonics brings these isolated continents into contact, the different species will compete for similar food and environments and typically only the strongest survive.

The position of continents relative to the poles of the Earth can also influence climate, evolution, and extinction. At times (like the present) when a continent is sitting on one or both of the poles, these continents tend to accumulate snow and ice and to become heavily glaciated. This causes ocean currents to become colder, lowers global sea levels, and reflects more of the sun's radiation back to space. Together, these effects can put a large amount of stress on species, inducing or aiding extinction.

The History of Life

Life on Earth has evolved from simple organisms known as archaea that appeared 3.85 billion years ago. Life may have been here earlier, but the record is not preserved, and the method by which life first appeared is also unknown and the subject of much thought and research by scientists, philosophers, and religious scholars.

The archaea derive energy from breaking down chemical bonds of carbon dioxide, water, and nitrogen and have survived to this day in environments where they are not poisoned by oxygen. They presently live around hot vents around mid-ocean spreading centers, deep in the ground in pore spaces between soil and mineral grains, and in hot springs. The archaea represent one of the three main branches of life, the other two branches being bacteria and eukarya. The plant and animal kingdoms are part of eukarya.

Prokaryotic bacteria (single-celled organisms lacking a cell nucleus) were involved in photosynthesis 3.5 billion years ago, gradually transforming atmospheric carbon dioxide to oxygen and setting the stage for the evolution of simple eukaryotes in the Proterozoic (containing a cell nucleus and membrane bound organelles). Two and half billion years later, by 1 billion years ago, cells began reproducing sexually. This long-awaited step allowed cells to exchange and share genetic material, speeding up evolutionary changes by orders of magnitude.

Oxygen continued to build in the atmosphere, and some of this oxygen was combined to make ozone. Ozone forms a layer in the atmosphere that blocks ultraviolet rays from the Sun, forming an effective shield against this harmful radiation. When the ozone shield became thick enough to block a large portion of the ultraviolet radiation, life began to migrate out of the deep parts of the ocean and land soils, into shallow water and places exposed to the sun. Multicellular life evolved around 670 million years ago, around the same time that the supercontinent of Gondwana was forming near the equator. Most of the planet's landmasses were joined together for a short while and then began splitting up and drifting apart around 550 million years ago. This breakup of the supercontinent of Gondwana is associated with the most remarkable diversification of life in the history of the planet. In a remarkably short period of no longer than 40 million years, life developed complex forms with hard shells and an incredible number of species appeared for the first time. This period of change marked the transition from the Precambrian era to the Cambrian period marking the beginning of the Paleozoic era. The remarkable development of life in this period is known as the Cambrian explosion. In the past 540 million years since the Cambrian explosion, life has continued to diversify with many new species appearing.

The Geologic Timescale

Era	Period	Epoch	Age (millions of years)	First Life-forms	Geology
		Holocene	0.01		
	Quaternary				
		Pleistocene	3	Humans	Ice age
Cenozoic		Pliocene	11	Mastodons	Cascades
		Neogene			
		Miocene	26	Saber-toothed tigers	Alps
	Tertiary	Oligocene	37		
		Paleogene			
		Eocene	54	Whales	
		Paleocene	65	Horses, Alligators	Rockies
	Cretaceous		135		
				Birds	Sierra Nevada
Mesozoic	Jurassic		210	Mammals	Atlantic
				Dinosaurs	
	Triassic		250		
	Permian		280	Reptiles	Appalachians
	Pennsylvanian		310		Ice age
				Trees	
	Carboniferous				
Paleozoic	Mississippian		345	Amphibians	Pangaea
				Insects	
	Devonian		400	Sharks	
	Silurian		435	Land plants	Laursia
	Ordovician		500	Fish	
	Cambrian		544	Sea plants	Gondwana
				Shelled animals	
			700	Invertebrates	Rodinia
Proterozoic			2500	Metazoans	
			3500	Earliest life	
Archean			4000		Oldest rocks
			4600		Meteorites

Geologic timescale showing history of life with major extinction events, some of which may have been aided by periods of massive volcanism from flood basalt provinces.

The evolution of life-forms is also punctuated with the extinction of many species, some as isolated cases, and others that die off at the same time as many other species in the rock record. There are a number of distinct horizons representing times when hundreds, thousands, and even more species suddenly died, being abundant in the record immediately before the formation of one rock layer and absent immediately above that layer, forever. Mass extinctions are typically followed, after several million years, by the appearance of many new species and the expansion and evolution of old species that did not go extinct. These rapid changes are probably a response to availability of environmental niches vacated by the extinct organisms. The new species rapidly populate these available spaces.

Mass extinction events are thought to represent major environmental catastrophes on a global scale. In some cases these mass extinction events can be tied to specific likely causes, such as meteorite impacts or massive volcanism, but in others their cause is unknown. Understanding the triggers of mass extinctions has important and obvious implications for ensuring the survival of the human race.

Examples of Mass Extinctions

Most species are present on Earth for about 4 million years. Many species come and go during background level extinctions and evolution of new species from old, but the majority of changes occur during the distinct mass dyings and repopulation of the environment. The Earth's biosphere has experienced five major and numerous less-significant mass extinctions in the past 500 million years (in the Phanerozoic era). These events occurred at the end of the Ordovician, in the Late Devonian, at the Permian-Triassic boundary, the Triassic-Jurassic boundary, and at the Cretaceous-Tertiary boundary.

The early Paleozoic saw many new life-forms emerge in new environments for the first time. The Cambrian explosion led to the development of trilobites, brachiopods, conodonts, mollusks, echinoderms, and ostracods. Bryozoans, crinoids, and rugose corals joined the biosphere in the Ordovician, and reef-building stromatoporoids flourished in shallow seas. The end-Ordovician extinction is one of the greatest of all Phanerozoic time. About half of all species of brachiopods and bryozoans died off, and more than 100 other families of marine organisms disappeared forever.

The cause of the mass extinction at the end of the Ordovician appears to have been largely tectonic. The major landmass of Gondwana had been resting in equatorial regions for much of the Middle Ordovician, but migrated toward the South Pole at the end of the Ordovician. This caused global cooling and glaciation, lowering sea levels from the high stand they had been resting at for most of the Cambrian and Ordovician. The combination of cold climates with lower sea levels, leading to a loss of shallow shelf environments for habitation, probably was enough to cause the mass extinction at the end of the Ordovician.

The largest mass extinction in history occurred at the Permian-Triassic boundary, over a period of about five million years. The Permian world included abundant corals, crinoids, bryozoans, and bivalves in the oceans and on land amphibians wandered about amid lush plant life. Ninety percent of oceanic species became extinct and 70 percent of land vertebrates died off at the end of the Permian. This greatest catastrophe did not have a single cause, but reflects the combination of various elements.

First, plate tectonics was again bringing many of the planet's landmasses together in a supercontinent (this time, Pangaea), causing greater competition for fewer environmental niches by Permian life-forms. The rich continental shelf areas were drastically reduced. As the continents collided, mountains were pushed up, reducing the effective volume of the continents available to displace the sea, so sea levels fell, putting additional stress on life by further limiting the availability of favorable environmental niches. The global climate became dry and dusty, and the supercontinent formation led to widespread glaciation. This lowered the sea level even more, lowered global temperatures, and put many life-forms in a very uncomfortable position. Many perished.

In the final million years of the Permian, the Northern Siberian plains let loose a final devastating blow. The Siberian flood basalts began erupting 250 million years ago, becoming the largest-known outpouring of continental flood basalts ever. Carbon dioxide was released in hitherto unknown abundance, warming the atmosphere and melting the glaciers. Other gases were also released, perhaps including methane, as the basalts probably melted permafrost and vaporized thick accumulations of organic matter that accumulate in high latitudes like that at which Siberia was located 250 million years ago. Massive volcanism therefore played a major role in one of the largest mass extinction events in the history of life on Earth.

The global biosphere collapsed, and evidence suggests that the final collapse happened in less than 200,000 years, and perhaps in less than 30,000 years. Entirely internal processes may have caused the end-Permian extinction, although some scientists now argue that an impact may have dealt the final deathblow. After it was over, new life-forms populated the seas and land, and these Mesozoic organisms tended to be more mobile and adept than their Paleozoic counterparts. The great Permian extinction created opportunities for new life-forms to occupy now-empty niches, and the most adaptable and efficient organisms took control. The toughest of the marine organisms survived, and a new class of land animals grew to new proportions and occupied the land and skies. The Mesozoic, time of the great dinosaurs, had begun.

The Triassic-Jurassic extinction is not as significant as the Permian-Triassic extinction. Mollusks were abundant in the Triassic shallow marine realm, with fewer brachiopods, and ammonoids recovered from near-total extinction at the Permian-Triassic boundary. Sea urchins became abundant and new groups of hexacorals replaced the rugose corals. Many land plants survived the end-Permian extinction, including the ferns and seed ferns that became abundant in the Jurassic. Small mammals that survived the end-Permian extinction rediversified in the Triassic, many to only become extinct at the close of the Triassic. Dinosaurs evolved quickly in the late Triassic, starting off small and attaining sizes approaching 20 feet (6.7 m) by the end of the era. The giant pterosaurs were the first-known flying vertebrate, appearing late in the Triassic. Crocodiles, frogs, and turtles lived along with the dinosaurs. The end of the Triassic is marked by a major extinction in the marine realm, including total extinction of the conodonts and a mass extinction of the mammal-like reptiles known as therapsids and the placodont marine reptiles. Although the causes of this major extinction event are poorly understood, the timing is coincident with the breakup of Pangaea and the formation of major evaporite and salt deposits. It is likely that this was a tectonic-induced extinction, with supercontinent breakup initiating new oceanic circulation patterns and new temperature and salinity distributions.

After the Triassic-Jurassic extinction, dinosaurs became extremely diverse and many quite large. Birds first appeared at the end of the Jurassic. The Jurassic was the time of the giant dinosaurs, which experienced a partial extinction affecting the largest varieties of Stegosauroids, Sauropods, and the marine Ichthyosaurs and Plesiosaurs. This extinction is also poorly explained, but may be related to global cooling. The other abundant varieties of dinosaurs continued to thrive through the Cretaceous.

The Cretaceous-Tertiary extinction is perhaps the most famous of mass extinctions because the dinosaurs perished during this event. The Cretaceous land surface of North America was occupied by bountiful species, including herds of dinosaurs both large and small, some herbivores and some carnivores. Other vertebrates included crocodiles, turtles, frogs, and several types of small mammals. The sky had flying dinosaurs including the vulturelike pterosaurs and insects including giant dragonflies. The dinosaurs had dense vegetation to feed on, including the flowering angiosperm trees, tall grasses, and many other types of trees and flowers. Life in the ocean had evolved to include abundant bivalves including clams and oysters, ammonoids, and corals that built large reef complexes.

Near the end of the Cretaceous, though the dinosaurs and other life-forms did not know it, things were about to change. High sea levels produced by mid-Cretaceous rapid seafloor spreading were falling, decreasing environmental diversity, cooling global climates, and creating environmental stress. Massive volcanic outpourings in the Deccan traps and the Seychelles formed as the Indian Ocean rifted apart and magma rose from an underlying mantle plume. Huge amounts of greenhouse gases were released, raising temperatures and stressing the environment. Many marine species were going extinct and others became severely stressed. Then one bright day, a visitor from space about 6 miles (10 km) across slammed into the Yucatán Peninsula of Mexico, instantly forming a fireball 1,200 miles (2,000 km) across, followed by giant tsunamis perhaps thousands of feet tall. The dust from the fireball plunged the world into a dusty fiery darkness, months or years of freezing temperatures, followed by an intense global warming. Few species handled the environmental stress well, and more than one-quarter of all the plant and animal kingdom families including 65 percent of all species on the planet became extinct forever. Gone were dinosaurs, mighty rulers of the Triassic, Jurassic, and Cretaceous. Oceanic reptiles

WALTER ALVAREZ
(1940–   )

In 1980, Walter Alvarez, along with coworkers who included his father, the Nobel Prize–winning physicist Luis Alvarez, located a thin layer of sediment associated with the boundary between the Cretaceous and Tertiary periods in Italy. This clay layer was deposited at a time that exactly correlated with the mass extinctions now known as the Cretaceous-Tertiary boundary, when the dinosaurs went extinct. Alvarez and his coworkers found the sample to be extremely enriched with iridium, a rare element in Earth's crust. Subsequent research showed the iridium layer at this time interval to be worldwide in extent. Although iridium is rare in Earth's crust, it is strongly enriched in many types of asteroids and meteorites. Therefore, Walter Alvarez and his coworkers proposed that the mass extinctions at the Cretaceous-Tertiary boundary were caused when a large body, such as an asteroid or meteorite, enriched in iridium struck Earth and produced great clouds of dust that obscured the Sun for several years.

This work has been written up in many scientific journals and also in the popular book *T-Rex and the Crater of Doom*. Alvarez is the recipient of numerous awards and honors, including the prestigious 2006 Nevada Medal and the Penrose Medal, the Geological Society of America's highest award. In 2005, he received a doctorate in geological sciences from the University of Siena in Italy.

and ammonoids died off, and 60 percent of marine planktonic organisms went extinct. The great Cretaceous-Tertiary dyings affected not only the numbers of species, but also the living biomass—the death of so many marine plankton alone amounted to 40 percent of all living matter on Earth at the time. Similar punches to land-based organisms decreased the overall living biomass on the planet to a small fraction of what it was before the Cretaceous-Tertiary knockout blows.

Some evidence suggests that the planet is undergoing the first stages of a new mass extinction. In the past 100,000 years, the ice ages have led to glacial advances and retreats, sea level rises and falls, the appearance and rapid explosion of human populations, and the mass extinction of many large mammals. In Australia, 86 percent of large (greater than 100 pounds) animals have become extinct in the past 100,000 years, and, in South America, North America, and Africa, the extinction is an alarming 79 percent, 73 percent, and 14 percent. This ongoing mass extinction appears to be the result of cold climates and, more important, predation and environmental destruction by humans. The loss of large-bodied species in many cases has immediately followed the arrival of humans in the region, with the clearest examples being found in Australia, Madagascar, and New Zealand. Similar loss of races through disease and famine has accompanied many invasions and explorations of new lands by humans.

The Future

Humans are experiencing a population explosion that cannot be sustained by the planet's limited resources. Very soon, freshwater and food sources will not be able to sustain the global population, and hunger, famine, disease, and war will follow. Can this fate be controlled? People are migrating in huge numbers to hazard-prone areas including coastlines, river flood plains, and the flanks of active volcanoes. Natural geologic hazards in these areas will cause disasters, and thousands of people will die. Perhaps greater understanding of natural geologic hazards will cause people to move to safer areas or to be better prepared for the hazards in the areas in which they live.

Why has the population of the human race exploded so dramatically? About 1 million years ago, there are estimated to have been a few thousand migratory humans on the Earth and by about 10,000 years ago this number had increased to only 5–10 million. It was not until about 8,000 years ago when humans began stable agricultural practices and domesticated some species of animals that the population rate started to increase substantially. The increased standards of living and

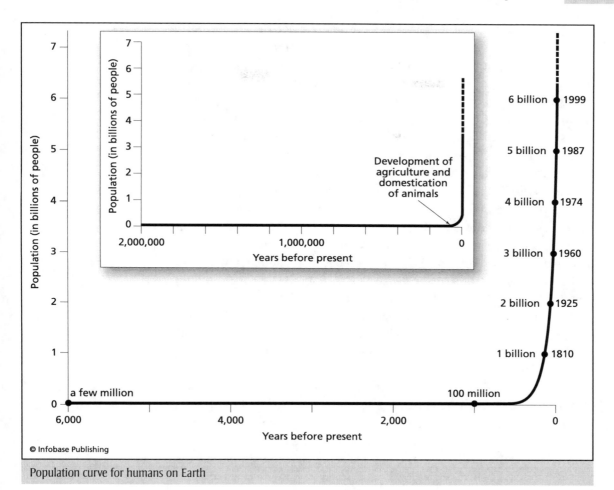

Population curve for humans on Earth

© Infobase Publishing

nutrition caused the population growth to soar to about 200 million by 2,000 years ago and 100 million by 1,000 years ago. By the 18th century, humans began manipulating their environments more, began public health services, and began to recognize and seek treatments for diseases that were previously taking many lives. The average life span began to soar, and world population surpassed 1 billion in the year 1810. A mere 100 years later, world population doubled again to 2 billion and had reached 4 billion by 1974. World population is now close to 7 billion and climbing more rapidly than at any time in history, doubling every 50 years. This rate of growth is not sustainable. At this rate, in about 800 years, there will be one human for every three square feet on Earth!

What will humans do when the population exceeds the ability of the Earth to support them? Perhaps there will be fighting and wars as with past isolated societies that reached their capacity to be supported by the land's natural resources. Alternatively, maybe humans will succumb to disease and famine, perhaps induced by drought. It is possible that a huge natural disaster such as an impact from outer space may send the human race back to a small fraction of the current population. Alternatively, the population rate could decrease in response to cultural changes. Some evidence suggests that the population growth rate is decreasing in developed countries and continues to rise in undeveloped and third-world countries. This could be in response to increased medical care reducing the need to have many children to ensure that some survive to adulthood or it could be a reflection of increased opportunities for women in developed societies.

Humans are causing mass extinction on a global scale that rivals the mass extinctions caused by massive flood basalt volcanism and meteorite impacts. Thousands of species are vanishing every year. Familiar to many is the rapid global decline in amphibians, particularly the frogs, in the past 30 years. Frogs could represent the proverbial canary in the coal mine, warning that changes in the environment are exceeding the limits to sustain certain kinds of life on the planet. Humans are destroying environments through uncontrolled population growth competing for limited resources, perhaps contributing to rapid decrease in global diversity. People are destroying many of the organisms that may be crucial to survival of the race, perhaps without even knowing it. Interrelationships between different organisms are complex. Humans may find themselves at the point of some day realizing that the simple bacteria that went extinct or the fungi that disappeared a few years back were essential for some process needed to survive, such as removing some greenhouse gas from the atmosphere. Rarely does one change in the environment go without consequence. Death of one species may allow another to expand, and this new species may be a predator to a third or carry parasites that can wipe out large segments of the population. Exponential population growth is hazardous and could be the ultimate demise of the human race.

Conclusion

The history of life on Earth is characterized by a model called punctuated equilibrium, where species suddenly appear, exist with relatively few changes for long periods of geological time, then suddenly become extinct over an extremely short time. After the extinction event, new forms of life emerge to fill the niches vacated by the extinct forms.

Research shows that many of these mass extinction events are correlated with a sequence of three events, including first an environmental stress caused by plate tectonic motions or climate cycles, then typically a larger environmental stress caused by a massive global volcanic event. This event typically plunges the planet into a deep cold or sometimes warm climate, stressing or causing many species to become extinct. For mass extinction events, a third event typically finishes off large parts of the global biomass—when a large meteorite or asteroid hits the Earth in a time period when the environment is stressed, it is usually more than most of the planet's life-forms can bear, and a mass extinction event results. Thus, plate tectonics, massive global volcanism, and impacts from space all play major roles in the evolution of life on Earth.

Summary

I gneous rocks are classified based on their composition and their texture. Mafic igneous rocks have about 50 percent silica, intermediate igneous rock 60 percent, and felsic 70 percent. If igneous rocks with these compositions have extrusive or volcanic textures they are called basalt, andesite, and rhyolite, respectively. Igneous rocks with similar compositions that cool and solidify below the surface are called plutonic, and the corresponding plutonic rocks are called gabbro, granodiorite, and granite. The mafic igneous rocks intrude or extrude at high temperatures, typically greater than 1,800°F (1,000°C), whereas felsic rocks tend to extrude at much lower temperatures of less than 1,135°F (600°C). Both mafic and felsic magmas may have a wide range in the amount of dissolved water that largely determines how explosive any volcanic eruption from that magma will be. The amount of dissolved water is related to the plate tectonic setting in which the magmas form.

The nature and style of volcanic eruptions is closely related to the plate tectonic setting in which the volcanic rock erupts. Extensional plate boundaries in the oceans are characterized by the greatest volume of volcanism on the Earth, yet these volcanic rocks erupt almost entirely under water at mid-ocean ridges, are nonexplosive, and pose little threat to people. The gases released to the ocean and atmosphere from mid-ocean ridge volcanism are however very significant in regulating global climate. Volcanism at convergent plate boundaries can be extremely explosive since the magmas in this tectonic setting are derived from fluids that escape from subducting oceanic crust and may contain large amounts of dissolved water and other gases. Convergent margin volcanoes have produced some of the most violent and deadly eruptions of recorded history, directly killing hundreds of thousands of people and indirectly accounting for millions of deaths through disease and famine brought on as a consequence of massive eruptions.

Volcanic eruptions are associated with a number of specific types of hazards that pose different levels of risk to populations. Lava flows move with variable speeds and can overrun villages and towns, but most people are able to walk away from moving lava flows without being injured. Pyroclastic flows including hot glowing avalanches known as nuée ardents are at the opposite end of the spectrum, as these types of flows result from explosive volcanism where tall eruption columns rise from a volcanic vent, then collapse sending very hot (typically 1,800°F [1,000°C]) walls of ash and rock screaming downhill at velocities of hundreds of miles per hour. Anything or anyone caught in the path of a nuée ardent is certain to be destroyed or killed. Other volcanoes have quietly emitted giant bubbles of dense carbon dioxide gas that move downhill, suffocating anything alive in their path that requires oxygen. Volcanic eruptions have initiated giant tsunami that have killed tens of thousands of people, and many eruptions are associated with earthquakes that serve both as a warning of impending eruptions and can be destructive in their own right. Some of the major eruptions of recorded history have vented large volumes of carbon dioxide, aerosols, and other gases into the atmosphere, with consequences to global climate. Volcanic eruptions can both lower global temperatures or lead to global warming depending on the substance released from the volcano and where in the atmospheric circulation system this material is placed.

Careful mapping of the ancient deposits around a volcano can help scientists predict what future eruptions may be like. Volcanoes with a history of mild eruptions are likely to continue with this trend, whereas a volcano with a past history of producing massive explosive eruptions is more likely to produce massive eruptions in the future. Programs to monitor the activity and threat from any volcano should incorporate this past history and monitor any changes in earthquake activity, bulging, or any shape changes of the volcano, changes in the emission of gases, temperature, or other electrical signal that could indicate an impending eruption. People who live near active volcanoes should be aware of the specific threats posed by these mountains, be aware of different levels of threat posed by different warnings, and have evacuation plans in place in the event of a volcanic emergency.

Examination of some of the greatest historical eruptions and some well-monitored recent eruptions shows the wide range in types of phenomena associated with volcanism. The eruption of Thera in Greece 3,650 years ago produced a tsunami that wiped out the coastal Minoan civilization, covered much of the Middle East with a dark ash cloud for days, and may account for many biblical legends. In 79 C.E., Mount Vesuvius buried the towns of Pompeii and Herculaneum in Italy, where more recently archaeologists have been able to uncover the horrors of a population suddenly buried by ash clouds that descended from a collapsing Plinian eruption column. Two of the greatest volcanic eruptions of modern history have been recorded from Tambora and Krakatau in Indonesia, which erupted in 1815 and 1883. Both of these eruptions were associated with the production of giant eruption columns, large atmospheric shock waves that traveled around the world, and phenomena such as earthquakes and tsunami that swept nearby villages killing tens of thousands of people. The eruption of Mount Pelée in Martinique is a tragedy that was amplified by desires of political power, domination, and ignorance of the threats posed by convergent margin volcanoes. Despite the growing activity of Mount Pelée, tens of thousands of people were forbidden to leave the island of Martinique before the local elections, and when a massive eruption buried the town of Saint-Pierre, nearly 30,000 people perished under hot glowing avalanche deposits. More recent eruptions of Mount Pinatubo in the Philippines and Mount Saint Helens in Washington State have shown how volcano monitoring and warning systems can alert residents to the threat posed by volcanoes and help to get local governments to evacuate populations before the eruptions, saving thousands of lives. Other eruptions have been less destructive, such as the slow flow from Nyiragongo volcano in Congo in 2002, where a lava flow slowly buried the town of Goma, which later rebuilt at a higher level on top of the new flow.

Some volcanic events in the history of the planet have been so massive that the flows cover hundreds of thousands or even millions of square miles. These massive global volcanic events emit so much gas into the atmosphere that the global climate has been changed. At several times in Earth's history, these huge volcanic events have occurred when the global environment was already stressed or changing and many organisms have been on the verge of extinction. At a few times in the distant geological past, a globally stressed environment has been associated with massive volcanism and climate change and then an impact from an asteroid or meteorite has plunged the world into global winters, leading to mass extinction events. In this way, volcanism has been closely associated with the evolution of life on Earth and with other processes that have regulated and controlled the planet's environment through time.

Glossary

asthenosphere—Weak partially molten layer in the Earth beneath the lithosphere, extending to about 155 miles (250 km) depth. The lithosphere slides on this weak layer, enabling plate tectonics to happen.

basalt—The most common igneous rock of the oceanic crust is called basalt, and its subvolcanic or plutonic equivalent is called gabbro. The density of basalt is 3.0 g/cm³; its mineralogy includes plagioclase, clinopyroxene, and olivine.

body waves—Seismic waves that travel through the whole body of the Earth and move faster than surface waves. There are two types of body waves—P- or compressional waves and S-waves, shear or secondary waves. P-waves deform material through a change in volume and density and can pass through solids, liquids, and gases. The kind of movement associated with passage of a P-wave is a back and forth type of motion. Secondary waves change the shape of a material but not its volume. Only solids can transmit secondary waves, whereas liquids cannot. Secondary waves move material at right angles to the direction of wave travel and thus they consist of an alternating series of sideways motions.

caldera—A roughly circular or elliptical depression, often occupied by a lake, that forms when the rocks above a subterranean magma mass collapse into the magma during a cataclysmic eruption.

collision zone—A zone of uplifted mountains where two continental plates or magmatic arcs have collided as a result of subduction along a convergent plate boundary.

compressional waves—See **body waves.**

convergent boundaries—Places where two plates move toward each other, resulting in one plate sliding beneath the other when a dense oceanic plate is involved or collision and deformation, when continental plates are involved. These types of plate boundaries may have the largest of all earthquakes.

diapirism—A mechanism of intrusion of melts or semimolten rock, or even just mobile material such as salt, into surrounding country rock where the magma forcefully rises and pushes aside the country rock, and the country rock moves out and down to accommodate the rise of the magma. The intruding material is typically less dense than the surrounding country rock.

differentiation—The separation of one composition crystal or liquid from another, by processes that may include melting, crystallization, and removal of the phase from other parts of the system.

dike—Any tabular, parallel-sided igneous intrusion that generally cuts across layering in the surrounding country rocks.

divergent boundaries—Divergent boundaries or margins are where two plates move apart, creating a void that is typically filled by new oceanic crust that wells up to fill the progressively opening hole.

earthquake—A sudden release of energy from slip on a fault, an explosion, or other event that causes the ground to shake and vibrate, associated with passage of waves of energy released at its source. An earthquake originates in one place and then spreads out in all directions along the fault plane.

flood basalt—Thick sequences of basaltic lava that cover very large areas of the continents or oceans are known as flood basalts, traps, or large igneous provinces.

geothermal gradient—A measure of how the temperature changes with increasing depth in the Earth.

granite, granodiorite—Common igneous rock types in the continental crust. The density of granodiorite is 2.6 g/cm^3; its mineralogy includes quartz, plagioclase, biotite, and some potassium feldspar. Granite has more quartz than granodiorite. The volcanic or extrusive equivalent of granite is rhyolite; the volcanic or extrusive equivalent of granodiorite is andesite.

hot spot—An area of unusually active magmatic activity that is not associated with a plate boundary. Hot spots are thought to form above a plume of magma rising from deep in the mantle.

hypabyssal—A type of intrusive rock that intrudes and crystallizes at shallow crustal levels, in between plutonic and volcanic in character.

igneous rocks—Rocks that have crystallized from a molten state known as magma. These include plutonic rocks, crystallized below the surface, and volcanic rocks, that have crystallized at the surface.

island arc—See **magmatic arc.**

jökulhlaups—Floods induced by volcanic eruptions beneath glaciers.

kimberlite—An unusual volcanic rock containing mixtures of material derived from the upper mantle and complex water-rich magmas. Many kimberlites intrude explosively, forming large pipes that fill with the magma and many contain diamonds.

lahar—A mudflow formed by the mixture of volcanic ash and water. Lahars are common on volcanoes, both during and for years after major eruptions.

lava—Magma, or molten rock, that flows at the surface of the Earth.

lithosphere—Rigid outer shell of the Earth that is about 75 miles (125 km) thick under continents and 45 miles (75 km) thick under oceans. The basic theorem of plate tectonics is that the lithosphere of the Earth is broken into about 12 large rigid blocks or plates that are all moving relative to one another.

magma—Molten rock, at high temperature, is called magma. When magma flows on surface it is known as lava.

magmatic arc—A line of volcanoes and igneous intrusions that forms above a subducting oceanic plate along a convergent margin is called a magmatic arc. Island arcs are built on oceanic crust, and continental margin magmatic arcs are built on continental crust.

mass extinction—When large numbers of different species of life on Earth all go extinct in a relatively short time, the event is called a mass extinction. Many mass extinctions can be shown to have occurred in less than a million or two years.

mass wasting—The movement of material downhill without the direct involvement of water.

mid-ocean ridge system—A 40,000-mile- (65,000-km-) long mountain ridge that runs through all the major oceans on the planet. The mid-ocean ridge system includes vast outpourings of young lava on the ocean floor and represents places where new oceanic crust is being generated by plate tectonics.

nuée ardent—A fast-moving glowing hot cloud of ash that can move down the flanks of volcanoes at hundreds of miles per hour during eruptions. Nuée ardents have been responsible for tens of thousands of deaths during eruptions.

partial melting—The process where a rock melts by only a small percentage, leaving mostly hot solid rock with a bit of (up to 10 or 20 percent) liquid. These melts may stay in place or move away to form larger magma bodies.

passive margin—A boundary between continental and oceanic crust that is not a plate boundary, characterized by thick deposits of sedimentary rocks. These margins typically have a flat shallow water shelf, then a steep drop-off to deep ocean floor rocks away from the continent.

peridotite—A common rock of the Earth's mantle. The average upper mantle composition is equivalent to peridotite. The density of peridotite is 3.3 g/cm^3; its mineralogy includes olivine, clinopyroxene, and orthopyroxene.

pillow lava—A form of lava flow with bulb- or pillowlike shapes, generally basaltic in composition, that forms beneath water and is common on the ocean floor.

plate tectonics—A model that describes the process related to the slow motions of more than a dozen rigid plates of solid rock on the surface of the Earth. The plates ride on a deeper layer of partially molten material that is found at depths starting at 60–200 miles (100–320 km) beneath the surface of the continents and 1–100 miles (1–160 km) beneath the oceans.

Plinian—A type of volcanic eruption characterized by a large and tall eruption column, typically reaching tens of thousands of feet into the air. Named after Pliny the Elder, from his description of Vesuvius.

plutonic—An igneous rock that has crystallized below the surface. Typically characterized by coarse grain size and forming large intrusive bodies known as plutons.

pyroclasts—Individual particles ejected during volcanic eruptions. May consist of volcanic bombs, country rock, or other particles.

rifts—Elongate topographic depressions, typically with faults along their margins, where the entire thickness of the lithosphere has ruptured in extension. These are places where the continents are beginning to break apart and, if successful, may form new ocean basins.

Ring of Fire—The informal name for the many chains of volcanic arcs that form a ring around the Pacific Ocean, including the west coasts of South and North America, Alaska, Kamchatka, Japan, and Indonesia.

seafloor spreading—The process of producing new oceanic crust, as volcanic basalt pours out of the depths of the Earth, filling the gaps generated by diverging plates. Beneath the mid-ocean ridges, magma rises from depth in the mantle and forms chambers filled with magma just below the crest of the ridges. The magma in these chambers erupts through cracks in the roof of the chambers and forms extensive lava flows on the surface. As the two different plates on either side of the magma chamber move apart, these lava flows continuously fill in the gap between the diverging plates, creating new oceanic crust.

seismograph—A device built to measure the amount and direction of shaking associated with earthquakes.

shear waves—See **body waves.**

slump—A type of mass wasting where a large mass of rock or sediment moves downward and outward along an upward curving fault surface. Slumps may occur undersea or on the land surface.

subduction—The destruction of oceanic crust and lithosphere by sinking back into the mantle at the deep ocean trenches. As the oceanic slabs go down, they experience higher temperatures that cause rock melts or magmas to be generated, which then move upward to intrude the overlying plate. Since subduction zones are long narrow zones where large plates are being subducted into the mantle, the melting produces a long line of volcanoes above the down-going plate and forms a volcanic arc. Depending on what the overriding plate is made of, this arc may be built on either a continental or on an oceanic plate.

subsidence—Sinking of one surface, such as the land, relative to another surface, such as sea level.

supercontinent—When plate tectonics and continental drift bring many or most of the planet's landmasses into continuity as one large continent, the continent is called a supercontinent. Examples of supercontinents include Pangaea that existed from about 300–200 million years ago and Gondwana that formed about 600 million years ago.

tephra—A general term for all ash and rock fragments strewn from a volcano.

transform boundaries—Places where two plates slide past each other, such as along the San Andreas Fault in California, and often have large earthquakes are known as transform boundaries.

tsunami—A giant harbor or deepwater wave, with long wavelengths, initiated by submarine landslides, earthquakes, volcanic eruptions, or other causes that suddenly displaces large amounts of water. Tsunamis can be much larger than normal waves when they strike the shore and cause great damage and destruction.

viscosity—A measure of the resistance to flow. The more viscous a fluid is, the more resistant it is to flow.

volcanic arc—A line of volcanoes that forms above a subducting oceanic plate at a convergent boundary. See also **magmatic arc.**

Further Reading and Web Sites

BOOKS

Albritton, C. C. Jr. *Catastrophic Episodes in Earth History.* London, England: Chapman and Hale, 1989. This book discusses major extinction events and their causes.

Alvarez, W. *T Rex and the Crater of Doom.* Princeton, N.J.: Princeton University Press, 1997. This book is a popular well-written book about the extinction of the dinosaurs being caused by a meteorite impact from space.

Blong, R. J. *Volcanic Hazards, A Sourcebook on the Effects of Eruptions.* New York: Academic Press, 1984. This book discusses the geological hazards associated with volcanic eruptions.

Cohen, J. E. *How Many People Can the World Support?* New York: W. W. Norton and Co., 1995. This book presents data and trends in population growth and compares populations with global resources.

Dawson, J. B. *Kimberlites and Their Xenoliths.* New York: Springer-Verlag, 1980. This is a technical resource on kimberlites.

De Boer, J. Z., and D. T. Sanders. *Volcanoes in Human History, The Far Reaching Effects of Major Eruptions.* Princeton, N.J.: Princeton University Press, 2002. This book discusses the effects of volcanic eruptions on human populations.

Diamond, J. *Guns, Germs, and Steel, The Fates of Human Societies.* New York: W. W. Norton and Co., 1999. This is a fascinating book about various factors that change human civilizations, including volcanic eruptions.

Eldredge, N. *Fossils: The Evolution and Extinction of Species.* Princeton, N.J.: Princeton University Press, 1997. This is a technical source on paleontology and evidence for the evolution of species.

Fisher, R. V. *Out of the Crater: Chronicles of a Volcanologist.* Princeton, N.J.: Princeton University Press, 2000. In this easy-to-read book, readers can understand the activities of a volcanologist.

Fisher, R. V., G. Heiken, and J. B. Hulen. *Volcanoes: Crucibles of Change.*

Princeton, N.J.: Princeton University Press, 1998. This book discusses volcanoes and volcanic activity.

Francis, P. *Volcanoes, A Planetary Perspective.* Oxford, England: Oxford University Press, 1993. This book discusses the role of volcanoes in planetary processes such as magma budget, lithosphere-atmosphere interactions, and variations among volcanoes on the planet.

LaCroix, A. *La Montagne Pelée et ses eruptions.* Paris, France: Masson, 1904. In French, this is a classic description of the 1902 eruption of Mount Pelée, with many spectacular photographs.

MacDougall, J. D., ed. *Continental Flood Basalts,* Dordrecht, Germany: Kluwer Academic Publishers, 1988.

Mahoney, J. J., and M. F. Coffin, eds. *Large Igneous Provinces, Continental, Oceanic, and Planetary Flood Volcanism.* Washington D.C.: American Geophysical Union, 1997. This is a collection of technical papers on flood basalt provinces of the world.

Mannard, G. W. *The Surface Expression of Kimberlite Pipes.* Ottawa, Canada: Geological Association of Canada, 1968. Although old, this book shows how subtle the surface expression of kimberlite pipes reaching to the mantle can be. The book offers guides for exploration for diamonds.

Martin, P. S., and R. G. Klein, eds. *Quaternary Extinctions.* Tucson, Ariz.: University of Arizona Press, 1989. This book discusses Quaternary through the present extinction events, including the present and ongoing extinction of mammals.

Melosh, H. Jay. *Impact Cratering: A Geologic Process.* Oxford, England: Oxford University Press, 1988. The physics of processes associated with impact cratering are examined in this book, including an assessment of the early great impact event that is postulated to have formed the Moon.

Mitchell, R. H. *Kimberlites, Mineralogy, Geochemistry, and Petrology.* New York: Plenum Press, 1989. This technical source discusses the rock types and minerals found in kimberlites.

Newhall, C. G., and R. S. Punongbayan, eds. *Fire and Mud: Eruptions and Lahars of Mount Pinatubo, Philippines.* Seattle, Wash.: University of Washington Press, 1996. There are many descriptions and photographs from the spectacular eruptions of Mount Pinatubo in this book.

Poag, C. W. *Chesapeake Invader, Discovering America's Giant Meteorite Crater.* Princeton, N.J.: Princeton University Press, 1999. This book presents evidence for a meteorite crater that is mostly submerged beneath the waters of Chesapeake Bay.

Ponting, C. *A Green History of the World.* New York: St. Martin's Press, 1991. An environmental perspective on global issues.

Roberto S., and R. I. Tilling. *Monitoring and Mitigation of Volcano*

Hazards. New York: Springer, 1996. A technical discussion of techniques of volcano monitoring.

Robock, A., and C. Oppenheimer, eds. *Volcanism and the Earth's Atmosphere.* Washington D.C.: American Geophysical Union, 2003. This book discusses the effects of large volcanic eruptions on global atmospheric conditions.

Scarth, A. *Vulcan's Fury, Man Against the Volcano.* New Haven, Conn.: Yale University Press, 1999. A popular book on volcanic hazards, and the effects of eruption on communities.

Sepkoski, J. J. Jr. *Mass Extinctions in the Phanerozoic Oceans: A Review, In Patterns and Processes in the History of Life.* Amsterdam, The Netherlands: Springer-Verlaag, 1982. This book presents evidence for the causes of major extinctions in the rock record.

Simkin, T., and R. S. Fiske. *Krakatau 1883: The Volcanic Eruption and Its Effects.* Washington D.C.: Smithsonian Institution Press, 1993. This book presents descriptions of the effects of the eruption of Krakatau.

Stanley, S. M. *Earth and Life Through Time.* New York: W. H. Freeman and Co., 1986. A comprehensive examination of the history of life on Earth.

———. *Extinction.* New York: Scientific American Library, 1987. A concise examination of mass extinction events and their causes.

Verbeek, R. D. M. *Krakatau.* Batavia: Imprimerie de l'etat (in French), 1886. A classic work on the description of the historical eruption of Krakatau.

JOURNAL ARTICLES

Burke, Kevin. "Tectonic Evolution of the Caribbean." *Annual Reviews of Earth and Planetary Sciences* 16 (1988). This is a technical review paper that describes the geology of the ocean floor and islands of the Caribbean, a submarine plateau, or large igneous province.

Chang, K. "Planet or No, It's on to Pluto." *Science Times, The New York Times,* (Jan. 29, 2002). A discussion of the declassification of Pluto as a planet.

Chapman, C. R., and D. Morrison. "Impacts on the Earth by asteroids and comets: Assessing the hazard." *Nature* 367 (1994). This short paper examines the likelihood of asteroids and comets hitting the Earth.

Erwin, D. H. "The Permo-Traissic extinction." *Nature* 367 (1994). The paper examines the evidence for an impact origin for the Permian-Triassic extinction event.

Holloway, M. "Trying to tame the roar of deadly lakes." *The New York Times, Science Tuesday,* (Feb. 27, 2001). This article presents an examination of the causes of the deadly carbon dioxide eruptions from Lake Nyos in Cameroon in 1984 and 1986, and measures that are being taken to reduce the future threat from these lakes.

Lacey, M. "Tens of thousands flee a devastating volcano in Congo." *The New York Times* (Jan 19, 2002). Article on the eruption of Nyiragongo volcano in Congo, 2002.

McCormick, M. P., L. W. Thompson, and C. R. Trepte. "Atmospheric effects of the Mt. Pinatubo eruption." *Nature* 373 (1995). This article discusses the atmospheric and climate effects of large volcanic eruptions, using Mt. Pinatubo as an example.

Moores, Eldredge. "Pre-1 Ga (pre Rodinian) ophiolites: Their tectonic and environmental implications." *Geological Society of America Bulletin* 114 (2002). Eldredge Moores discusses the evidence for the formation of oceanic crust and large igneous provinces at times older than 1 billion years ago in this paper.

Rampino, M. R., S. Self, and R. B. Stothers. "Volcanic Winters." *Annual Reviews of Earth and Planetary Science* 16 (1988). This paper discusses the atmospheric effects of large volcanic eruptions.

Renne, P. R., Z. Zichao, M. A. Richards, M. T. Black, and A. R. Basu. "Synchrony and causal relations between Permian Triassic boundary crises and Siberian flood volcanism." *Science* 269 (1995). This paper suggests that eruption of a vast field of volcanic rocks in Siberia may have caused the major extinction event at the Permian-Triassic boundary.

Sharpton, V. L., and P. D. Ward. "Global Catastrophes in Earth History." *Geological Society of America Special Paper* 247 (1990). This review paper discusses major extinction events and how they may have been caused by impacts and volcanic eruptions.

Sheridan, M. F., and K. H. Wohletz. "Hydrovolcanism, Basic considerations and Review." *Journal of Volcanology and Geothermal Research* 17 (1983). This technical paper describes the phenomena of explosive water-rich volcanism.

Smith, A. L., and M. J. Roobol. "Mt. Pelée, Martinique; A study of an Active Island arc volcano." *Geological Society of America Memoir* 175 (1990). This paper presents the case that Mt. Pelée, Martinique, is still an active volcano and needs to be monitored carefully.

Wyllie, P. J. "The origin of kimberlite." *Journal of Geophysical Research* 85 (1980). This review paper presents a technical discussion on the different models for the origins of kimberlites.

INTERNET RESOURCES

In the past few years numerous Internet Web sites that have information about volcanoes have appeared. Most of these Web sites are free and include historical information about specific volcanoes, real-time monitoring of volcanic eruptions around the world, and educational material.

The sites listed below have interesting information and graphics about different volcanoes. This book may serve as a useful companion while surfing through the information on the internet when encountering unfamiliar phrases, terms, or concepts that are not fully explained on the Web site. The following list of Web sites is recommended to help enrich the content of this book and make your exploration of volcanoes and volcanic hazards more enjoyable. In addition, any eruptions that occur after this book goes to press will be discussed on these Web sites, so checking them can help you keep this book up to date. From these Web sites you will also be able to link to a large variety of volcano-related sites. Every effort has been made to ensure the accuracy of the information provided for these Web sites. However, due to the dynamic nature of the internet, changes might occur, and any inconvenience is regretted.

Alaska Volcano Observatory, United States Geological Survey. Available online. URL: http://www.avo.alaska.edu/ Accessed August 27, 2006. The Alaska Volcano Observatory (AVO) is a joint program of the United States Geological Survey (USGS), the Geophysical Institute of the University of Alaska Fairbanks (UAFGI), and the State of Alaska Division of Geological and Geophysical Surveys (ADGGS). AVO was formed in 1988, and uses federal, state, and university resources to monitor and study Alaska's hazardous volcanoes, to predict and record eruptive activity, and to mitigate volcanic hazards to life and property.

Brantley, Steve, and Bobbie Myers. United States Geological Survey. "Mount St. Helens—From the 1980 Eruption to 2000." Available online. URL: http://pubs.usgs.gov/fs/2000/fs036-00/ Accessed August 27, 2006. History of Mount Saint Helens Eruptions.

Cascades Volcano Observatory, United States Geological Survey. Available online. URL: http://vulcan.wr.usgs.gov/ Accessed August 27, 2006. The USGS's Cascades Volcano Observatory (CVO) strives to serve the national interest by helping people to live knowledgeably and safely with volcanoes and related natural hazards including earthquakes, landslides, and debris flows in the western United States and elsewhere in the world. CVO assesses hazards before they occur by identifying and studying past hazardous events. The CVO provides warnings during volcanic crises by intensively monitoring restless volcanoes and interpreting results in the context of current hazards assessments. They investigate and report on hazardous events after they occur to improve our assessment and prediction skills and to help develop new concepts of how volcanoes work. Their web site has information about individual volcanoes of the Cascades, news, current events, discussion of hazards, photo archives, and many educational links.

Dinosaur Extinction Page. Available online. URL: http://web.ukonline. co.uk/a.buckley/dino.htm. Accessed August 27, 2006. Web site offers short summaries of some theories of dinosaur extinction, including meteorite impacts and volcanic eruptions.

Dzurisin, Dan, Opater Stauffer, and James Hendley II. United States Geological Survey. "Living with Volcanic Risk in the Cascades." Available online. URL: http://pubs.usgs.gov/fs/1997/fs165-97/ Accessed August 27, 2006. General discussion of overall volcanic hazards in the Cascades, and links to other sites with more specific information.

Gardner, Cynthia, William Scott, Jon Major, and Thomas Pierson. United States Geological Survey. "Mount Hood—History and Hazards of Oregon's Most Recently Active Volcano." Available online. URL: http:// pubs.usgs.gov/fs/2000/fs060-00/ Accessed August 27, 2006. Discussion of historical activity of Mount Hood and possible hazards to Portland Oregon and vicinity. Includes maps of proximal and distal hazard areas.

Geological Survey of Canada. Available online. URL: http://www.unb. ca/passc/ImpactDatabase/ Accessed August 27, 2006. The Geological Survey of Canada has compiled an Earth Impact database, available at the site above. The Earth Impact Database is maintained as a not-for-profit source of information to assist the scientific, industrial, government, and public communities around the world in furthering our collective knowledge of impact structures on Earth. The database is regularly maintained and contains maps and images of various impact craters.

Global Volcanism Network, Museum of Natural History E-421, Smithsonian Institution. Available online. URL: http://www.volcano.si.edu/ Accessed August 27, 2006. The Global Volcanism Program (GVP) seeks better understanding of all volcanoes through documenting their eruptions—small as well as large—during the last 10,000 years. The range of volcanic behavior is great enough, and volcano lifetimes are long enough, that we must integrate observations of contemporary activity with historical and geological records of the recent past in order to prepare wisely for the future. By building a global framework of volcanism over thousands of years, and by stimulating documentation of current activity, the GVN attempts to provide a context in which any individual volcano's benefits and dangers can be usefully assessed. GVP also plays a central role in the rapid dissemination of information about ongoing volcanic activity on Earth by publishing eruption reports from local observers in the monthly Bulletin of the Global Volcanism Network.

Hawaiian Volcano Observatory. Available online. URL: http://hvo.wr.usgs. gov/ Accessed August 27, 2006. The Hawaiian Volcano Observatory (HVO) enjoys a worldwide reputation as a leader in the study of active volcanism. Due to their usually benign natures, Kilauea and Mauna Loa, the most active volcanoes on the Island of Hawaii, can be studied up close in relative safety. While observations made by 19th-century missionaries and travelers constitute a large part of the early and colorful history of volcano watching in Hawaii, HVO's origins are rooted in a desire to use scientific methodology to understand the nature of volcanic processes and to reduce their risks to society. HVO is part of the Volcano Hazards Program of the United States Geological Survey. Their staff conducts research on the volcanoes of Hawaii and works with emergency-response officials to protect people and property from earthquakes and volcano-related hazards. The HVO Web site includes updates of current volcanic activity, discussions of volcanic hazards, and a history of volcanic observations.

Hill, David, Roy Bailey, Michael Sorey, James Hendley II, and Peter Stauffer. United States Geological Survey. "Living with a Restless Caldera—Long Valley, California." Available online. URL: http://pubs. usgs.gov/fs/fs108-96/ Accessed August 27, 2006. Description of the rising magma beneath Long Valley, California, and the volcanic hazards this poses to the western United States. Includes accounts of historical eruptions and system of warnings that are in place in the event of an eruption.

Johnson, Jenda. United States Geological Survey. "Viewing Lava Safely—Common Sense is Not Enough." Available online. URL: http://pubs. usgs.gov/fs/2000/fs152-00/ Accessed August 27, 2006. A short guide to some of the volcanic hazards associated with viewing lava flows on Kilauea Volcano, Hawaii.

Lunar and Planetary Laboratory, University of Arizona. Available online. URL: http://seds.lpl.arizona.edu/nineplanets/nineplanets/meteorites. html Accessed August 27, 2006. Web site has extensive list of information about meteors, meteorites, impacts, and links to other sites. Site is run by the Students for the Exploration and Development of Space (SEDS).

NASA Ames Research Center. Available online. URL: http://impact.arc. nasa.gov// Accessed August 27, 2006. This Web site from NASA's Ames Research Center describes various hazards associated with asteroid and comet impacts with Earth.

Newhall, Chris, James Hendley II, and Peter Stauffer. United States Geological Survey. "Benefits of Volcano Monitoring Far Outweigh Costs—The Case of Mount Pinatubo." Available online. URL: http://pubs.usgs. gov/fs/1997/fs115-97/ Accessed August 27, 2006. Analysis of the methods, costs, and benefits of volcano monitoring at Mount Pinatubo.

Newhall, Chris, James Hendley II, and Peter Stauffer. United States Geological Survey. "The Cataclysmic 1991 Eruption of Mount Pinatubo,

Philippines." Available online. URL: http://pubs.usgs.gov/fs/1997/fs113- 97/ Accessed August 27, 2006. Detailed descriptions of the huge eruption of Mount Pinatubo in 1991. Also includes assessment of continuing hazards.

Newhall, Chris, Peter Stauffer, and James Hendley II. United States Geological Survey. "Lahars of Mount Pinatubo, Philippines." Available online. URL: http://pubs.usgs.gov/fs/1997/fs114-97/ Accessed August 27, 2006. Descriptions of the huge lahars and mudflows of Mount Pinatubo, and what the warning signs of impending lahars were.

Scott, Kevin, Wes Hildreth, and Cynthia Gardner. United States Geological Survey. "Mount Baker—Living with an Active Volcano." Available online. URL: http://pubs.usgs.gov/fs/2000/fs059-00/ Accessed August 27, 2006. Discussion of hazards associated with Mount Baker, and discussions of why certain areas have been closed to tourists.

Sorey, Michael, Chris Farrar, William Evans, David Hill, Roy Bailey, James Hendley II, and Peter Stauffer. United States Geological Survey. "Invisible CO_2 Gas Killing Trees at Mammoth Mountain, California." Available online. URL: http://pubs.usgs.gov/fs/fs172-96/ Accessed August 27, 2006. Fascinating account of how large volumes of CO_2 gas are seeping out of the caldera beneath Long Valley and Mammoth Mountain, California, and killing many trees in the area. This may indicate an impending eruption.

St. Louis University Center for Environmental Science. Available online. URL: http://CES.SLU.EDU. Accessed May 9, 2007. This site has discussions of many types of geologic hazards, including earthquakes, volcanoes, tsunami, hurricanes, and how these geologic phenomena are affecting people.

Sutton, Jeff, Tamar Elias, James Hendley II, and Peter Stauffer. United States Geological Survey. "Volcanic Air Pollution—A Hazard in Hawai'i." Available online. URL: http://pubs.usgs.gov/fs/fs169-97/ Accessed August 27, 2006. Discussion of the various gases and pollution produced by Kilauea volcano, Hawaii.

United States Geological Survey. "Living on Active Volcanoes—The Island of Hawai'i." Available online. URL: http://pubs.usgs.gov/fs/fs074-97/ Accessed August 27, 2006. Discussion of the volcanic activity and hazards on the island of Hawaii. Includes maps showing areas of low through high risk for volcanic hazards.

United States Geological Survey Volcano Hazards Program. Available online. URL: http://volcanoes.usgs.gov/ Accessed August 27, 2006. Contains updates of U.S. and worldwide volcanic activity and has feature articles on recent research. Also has links to sites on volcanic hazards, historical eruptions, monitoring programs, emergency planning and warning schemes. Has resources including photos, fact sheets, videos, and an education page. Also offers grants to college students doing volcano research.

Volcano Disaster Assistance Program. Available online. URL: http://pubs. usgs.gov/fs/1997/fs064-97/ Accessed August 27, 2006. This is a cooperative effort between the U.S. agency for International Development (Office of Foreign Disaster Assistance) and the US Geological Survey. These organizations head a mobile response team that has been mobilized many times since its initiation in 1986, saving numerous lives from areas at risk.

Volcanoworld. Available online. URL: http://volcano.und.edu/ Accessed August 27, 2006. Presents updated information about eruptions, volcanoes, and has many interactive pages designed for different grade levels from kindergarten through college and professional levels. Volcanoworld is an award-winning Web site, designed as a collaborative Higher Education, K-12, and Public Outreach project of the North Dakota and Oregon Space Grant Consortia administered by the Department of Geosciences at Oregon State University.

Index

Note: Page numbers in *italic* refer to illustrations, *m* indicates a map, *t* indicates a table.